KU-020-051

WHAT I TOLD MY DAUGHTER

LESSONS FROM LEADERS ON RAISING THE NEXT GENERATION OF EMPOWERED WOMEN

EDITED BY

Nina Tassler

WITH Cynthia Littleton

ATRIA PAPERBACK

NEW YORK LONDON TORONTO SYDNEY NEW DELHI

ATRIA
PAPERBACK

An Imprint of Simon & Schuster, Inc.
1230 Avenue of the Americas
New York, NY 10020

Copyright © 2016 by Jerry Levine, Inc.

All rights reserved, including the right to reproduce this book or portions thereof in any form whatsoever. For information, address Atria Books Subsidiary Rights Department, 1230 Avenue of the Americas, New York, NY 10020.

First Atria Paperback edition April 2017

ATRIA PAPERBACK and colophon are trademarks of Simon & Schuster, Inc.

For information about special discounts for bulk purchases, please contact Simon & Schuster Special Sales at 1-866-506-1949 or business@simonandschuster.com.

The Simon & Schuster Speakers Bureau can bring authors to your live event. For more information, or to book an event, contact the Simon & Schuster Speakers Bureau at 1-866-248-3049 or visit our website at www.simonspeakers.com.

Interior design by Kyoko Watanabe

Manufactured in the United States of America

10 9 8 7 6 5 4 3

Library of Congress Cataloging-in-Publication Data is available.

ISBN 978-1-4767-3467-5
ISBN 978-1-4767-3468-2 (pbk)
ISBN 978-1-4767-3469-9 (ebook)

902829010 9

WHAT I TOLD
MY DAUGHTER

For my husband, son, and daughter
Jerry, Matt, and Alice
And thank you to my mother, Norma

Contents

CONTENTS

CONTENTS

CONTENTS

Preface

I was forty when my daughter was born. After nine months, sixty pounds, and enough water retained to fill the Los Angeles reservoir I gave birth via emergency C-section to a ball of fire. This was not entirely surprising given the journey my husband, Jerry Levine, and I took to meet her.

I had gone through a festive assortment of fertility treatments ranging from the requisite menu of drugs and procedures to an experimental medical procedure that occurred entirely by accident; Dr. Richard Paulson flooded my uterus with my husband's sperm when one of my fertilized eggs decided to make a run for it while going through egg implantation. This was the second time I had gone through an in vitro experiment (I would remind myself periodically that I was still a lab rat). Lots of needles, lots of doctor appointments, all while climbing the high peak of Mt. Anxiety—and then seven to ten days later I got the thrill of taking a pregnancy test. Talk about torture. The wait for the results, the fantasy that I am, in the very moment I am about to take the call from the doctor, in fact, pregnant. How could he possibly give me bad news? Not going to happen, no way. I wasn't quite sure how to process the information the nurse was giving me over the phone—she reported numbers and levels and hormones.

"Am I pregnant?" I asked.

Politely, the nurse replied, "Probably not at these levels."

"What level do I need to hit, just give me a number, and I'll hit it, I'm very goal oriented," I said in my intense, type-A network executive voice. What a ridiculous thing to say—borderline crazy, I realize as soon as the words leave my mouth. The disappointment made my skin feel thick.

The following week Dr. Paulson, the kind, patient Lord of Fertility Manor, called me at home to see how I was feeling, physically and emotionally. I remember getting out of bed to answer the phone. He told me to take a break from the shots. Take a breather. Don't think about conception, return to sex without an agenda. Just relax. Okay. I hung up the phone and started to cry.

Two months later I was pregnant. Regular old sex. I think there were some survivors from the sperm invasion waiting for the perfect egg. They found her. Or rather she grabbed one by the scruff of his collar and commanded, "You!" as if she were Diana, the huntress of Roman mythology.

Our daughter was setting the stage for her arrival into the world from, literally, Day One. She dictated the terms of her insemination, and she was going to orchestrate every detail, from the pounds I gained during pregnancy to the trauma she and I went through after an induced labor resulting in a horrific emergency cesarean delivery.

A decade and a half later, I am just beginning to understand the significance of my daughter's creation and birth. We named her Alice Luisa after both of her great-grandmothers. Each of those women were heroes in their own right—the eldest children in both of their families, immigrants who came to the United States with little but grew up to be formidable women. We chose the name not just because Jewish tradition says naming your child for a deceased loved one allows their memory to be kept alive, but because Jerry and I hoped all the traits we admired in our grandmothers would be passed down to our daughter. It was a thoughtful and significant decision.

From the day she was born, I was committed to raising Alice as a feminist, just as I was by my mother. To me, that means understanding that women are in every respect the equals of men and should never in any circumstance be considered otherwise. I made a point of instilling these principles in my son, Matthew, when he was little. One morning on our drive to school he declared, "You know, Mom, boys are better than girls." I pulled the car over, turned off the engine, and made sure he saw the look on my face. "No, Matthew," I told him, "boys and girls are *different* but they are equal." This is an exchange that my son remembers to this day.

That deep-in-the-bones understanding of equality comes with the acknowledgment that we live in a patriarchal society that imposes gender distinctions in so many ways—from the toys we play with as toddlers to the careers we pursue to the roles we carve out in our own family structures. As women, we have a responsibility to combat such prejudice with our words and deeds, sometimes with our feet, and with fists clenched in solidarity. We don't need to demand equality so much as we need to live and breathe it in everything we do. It is an extra burden, one that women have shouldered since time immemorial.

At the core of what makes us women, the objectification of female sexuality has a profound influence on our psyches from our earliest days. In today's hyperactive media landscape, we are buffeted by an endless stream of messages to be prettier, thinner, sexier, lustier, happier, smarter but not too threatening. Ask any mother—you never feel the outrage about our cultural obsession with false ideals of beauty until you've seen it through the questioning eyes of your baby girl.

As my daughter reached her preteen years, I began a quest to hone my personal definition of feminism and learn how other women defined their strength. I read all the books and research I could find, but nothing quite answered the questions I had about the unique intimacy that exists between a mother and daughter. I wanted to know how other women communicated with their daughters, how they instilled in them the values and principles that matter most. I wanted to hear the humor, sense the subtext, and savor the lyrical language used in telling each story—women who are all so different from one another, and different from their mothers.

I realized that if I was searching for advice and inspiration on ways to teach girls to feel empowered, other moms probably were too. My instincts told me to reach out to women who are in leadership roles in a variety of disciplines, from Oscar- and Emmy-winning actresses to pioneering doctors and scientists to spiritual leaders, activists, politicians, academicians, writers, directors, business executives, and those who do heroic work with nonprofit and philanthropic organizations. I was overwhelmed by how quickly so many embraced the "What I Told My Daughter" concept.

On the journey of assembling this book, I came to understand that raising a daughter with feminist ideals is as much of a parental responsibility as it is to ensure that she eats a well-balanced diet and gets plenty of sleep. I remember the days when Alice was in preschool, and I would pack her backpack in the morning with snacks, water, hand wipes, and other items to get her through the day. I believe as mothers we need to pack our daughters' backpacks with the supplies necessary to be a strong, determined proponent of gender equality. We can't assume that she'll absorb these principles automatically, no matter how many wonderful role models she has in her life. We have to work at teaching those lessons.

My point of view on what it means to be an empowered woman came directly from my mother, Norma. She sang to me lullabies of freedom, celebrating our right to full equality with men within the broader context of the civil rights and antiwar movements of the 1960s. She instilled in me the fundamental belief that I was destined for some variation on greatness—and it was those ideals that gave me the underlying confidence and determination to pursue a career that has taken me to the top echelon of the entertainment business. My mother gave me the gift of never doubting that I would achieve my goals.

I was a young girl when the Vietnam War was at its height. I grew up in a small town in upstate New York, West Copake, where many local boys had been drafted and were serving overseas.

In the center of the town there was a large clock on a pedestal commemorating the men and women who served in World War II. The general feeling among the people in my town was to support the war—that's just what you did. It was almost unheard-of for people to protest our government's actions or express antiwar sentiments. So when I stood on crisp autumn nights by the base of that clock among a small group of concerned locals with a candle in one hand and my mother's in the other, I was afraid.

The setting itself was unnerving to a kid. It was dark. People were singing emotional antiwar songs; I was one of a few children surrounded by adults. I would sing softly as I knew all the words to "Blowin' in the Wind" and "Universal Soldier." But I felt alone, and I knew discussing the evening's activities the next day at school would not help my popularity. But as time went by, I grew less fearful. The strangeness I felt was replaced by the familiar and the conviction that I was doing something important. Perhaps I was getting comfortable with the sound of my own voice, or feeling that I was going to be part of a bigger story by helping to bring an end to a war a half a world away that was killing people from my town. Or maybe I grew more confident because my mother was beside me. It was as if she sent me secret signals through her firm grip of my hand. The message received was: "It's okay to stand alone, to be afraid, to hold unpopular beliefs, to hear the sound of your own voice and to let courage grow from within?"

These are the lessons my mother taught me with her words and with her inspiring example. Now with my own daughter I search for similar opportunities. Some days it feels more difficult as the fast pace and congestion of our daily lives seems to make it hard to even breathe.

But the experiences that help us raise strong, confident daughters are found everywhere, often when we least expect it. Reading these stories from an eminent group of women is a way to preserve and to share our collective wisdom with women around the world, for years to come.

The spark of inspiration for this book came to me at a most unexpected time and place: the Phoenix Convention Center, where I watched Alice, then thirteen, take part in a volleyball tournament that draws hundreds of young female players from all over the world.

I was struck at first by the sheer number of women gathered in one place for the purpose of demonstrating their athletic skills and all the leadership and character traits that come with team sports. This event, featuring players ranging in age from twelve to eighteen, was all about achievement, about striving to perform at the highest levels as individuals and as a collective unit. It was also an assault on the senses, what with the oppressive June heat (it was 115 degrees outside, literally), and the roar of the screeching, cheering, and ball-smacking sounds coming from row after row of volleyball courts erected in the cavernous space.

I'd never been in such a female-centric environment before. The energy radiating from the assembly of young girls and their mothers was electrifying. As I looked around, I saw a panorama of womanhood, in all shapes and sizes, from preteen middle schoolers to young women about to head off to college to all the mothers who guided them to this moment. I recognized that while we all had much in common, every mother and every daughter traveled their own path to get to this moment.

I didn't know it at the time, but that's when I made up

my mind to shepherd this book of deeply personal essays. As someone who has built a career on developing great storytellers, I believe every woman has an experience that can inspire and enlighten others.

At the volleyball tournament, my daughter's team didn't win their final match. But Alice played hard and was there for her teammates at pivotal points in the game. When I told her I was most impressed by how "consistent" her performance was, it was as if I had a magic key and unlocked a secret door, because I had given her an honest reflection that validated her own feelings. It wasn't just a platitude. I felt how much it meant to her that I'd noticed her contributions to the game.

In that moment, I could feel that my role in her life was shifting. We had turned a corner. We were starting to communicate on a more adult level than we ever had before. Alice was of the age where she no longer needed me to be there with Band-Aids when she scraped her knee; she needed me to be there with honest emotional support as she began to tackle adult-size challenges and opportunities. I was immensely proud of her for working so hard all season toward her goal, and I thought about all the ways I'd tried to instill that kind of drive and confidence in her.

The importance of heroes and role models was underscored during the tournament when the girls were addressed by volleyball star Misty May-Treanor. This was an inspiring moment, because May-Treanor is a rock star to these girls and her motivational words had great resonance. She was two months away from winning her third Olympic-career gold medal, this time at the 2012 summer games in London.

Weeks after the volleyball tournament, I was still so energized by the experience that I knew I had to make this book happen. I am deeply grateful to the busy women who took time out to contribute their stories. In the spirit of reaching out and giving back, a portion of the proceeds from this book will be donated to two organizations devoted to nurturing leadership skills in young women: Girls Inc. and the United Nations Foundation's Girl Up campaign.

Working on this book has been nothing less than a revelation for me. I never fully appreciated the strength of the emotional and intellectual foundation provided by my mother's teachings until the essays collected here gave me insights into the challenges that others have faced. Our contributors reflect the breadth of maternal experiences and the melting pot of racial, ethnic, sexual orientation, education, income levels, and cultural differences that define our country. The order of presentation in this book seeks to both accentuate that diversity and reinforce the universality of motherhood. Underneath the divisive labels that are often affixed to our jobs—working mom, tiger mom, helicopter mom, soccer mom, et cetera—we are all simply women trying to do our best to raise the next generation of empowered leaders. In a few instances, we offer the dual perspective of essays from mothers and their daughters.

Pat Benatar writes about being under enormous pressure from her record label to hide her pregnancy when she was topping the charts in the 1980s. Jehan Sadat, widow of Egyptian leader Anwar Sadat, recalls the extra hurdles she scaled to earn her doctorate degree in the face of accusations of favoritism from university officials. Dr. Susan Love, the eminent breast cancer expert, recounts the legal battle she waged with her wife, Helen Cooksey, to adopt their daughter, Katie. Dolores

Huerta, cofounder of the United Farm Workers union with Cesar Chavez, tells the story of leading a labor movement while scrambling every day to find child care for her own children.

Other contributors offer stories of mother-daughter experiences that range from funny to heartbreaking to uplifting. Marie Osmond reveals how she and her daughter wound up breaking off engagements virtually on the eve of walking down the aisle. Author Ayelet Waldman tells how "Be nice to the fat girls" became a family motto. Actress Christine Baranski describes how a muddy fall from a horse taught her daughter an important lesson. Brooke Shields writes candidly about how she turned scary encounters with paparazzi into a teachable moment for her girls.

The common thread in all of these tales is the extra layer of responsibility that mothers have to guide their daughters to be empowered, to be confident, and to make the right choices for them regardless of societal pressures.

From the time I was a girl, I never doubted that I had every right—dare I say even a sense of entitlement—to pursue the career of my dreams. It started with acting, which was an uphill battle for me no matter how much I loved the idea of being an actor. After a period of trial and error in my twenties, I found my natural strength as a program development executive, someone who works with writers, directors, and actors to help shape raw ideas and talent into prime-time TV series. Contrary to our public image, network "suits" aren't all meddling incompetents who do nothing but deliver nonsensical notes to writers. Television is an extremely tough business—the failure rate of new shows is higher than 80 percent for most TV networks. But when it works, nothing in entertainment packs more of a punch than a hit television series. These are the storytellers and the characters that Americans welcome into their living rooms (and nowadays their smartphones and tablets) week after week.

I've been fortunate in my career to have been involved with some of the biggest TV hits of the past few decades—from the dedicated doctors of *ER* to the forensic sleuths of *CSI* and its offshoots to the lovable geeks of *The Big Bang Theory*, among many other shows. I have been lucky to have been mentored by great bosses, male and female, and to have worked for progressive companies, notably Warner Bros., which has long reigned as the largest studio in Hollywood, and CBS, the "Tiffany Network." I am indebted to many predecessors in the entertainment industry who blazed the trails that allowed women to reach the highest ranks at networks and studios. In 2004, I took over the job of overseeing programming for CBS from the woman who previously held that position, Nancy Tellem, an accomplished executive who is one of the most respected strategic thinkers in all of media.

For more than twenty-five years, at CBS, Warner Bros., and Lorimar Productions, I had the privilege of working for an enlightened leader, CBS Corporation chairman, president, and CEO Leslie Moonves. Leslie and I enjoyed a longevity that is rare in the entertainment industry. We thrived together on the strength of a relationship built on trust, respect, and support, whether in success or failure. Finally, Leslie granted me the ultimate gift of controlling my own destiny as an executive. After much consideration, I made the decision to resign my post as chairman of CBS Entertainment in December 2015, just as we finished up work on this book. As much as I have loved working with writers, actors, directors, producers, and others in the creative community, assembling *What I Told My Daughter* helped me realize that it was time to seek new challenges and flex new muscles.

Through all my years in television, I have rarely felt disadvantaged because I'm a woman. Developing shows that appeal to a wide audience by definition means finding shows that connect with female viewers, because women make up a little more than half of the total viewing audience in the United States. Having a built-in sense of what distinct groups of women might respond to when they turn on the tube is only a plus in my business.

But like women in many lines of work, I have often walked into high-level meetings where I was the only female in the room. I've experienced the aggravation of being talked over by voices deeper than mine. I've had the demeaning experience of making a presentation or advocating a position only to have questions and comments directed to a male coworker. I stand about five foot two in low heels, which means that I sometimes have to work harder to exert my authority with unfamiliar people. Nowadays the stature I gained through my position at CBS mostly combats the problem of those who think, even subconsciously, that short equals weak. But some people still blurt out, "You're so tiny" or "You're not as tall as I thought you were," when I first meet them.

Dealing with this perception issue has made me more sensitive to how women are perceived and portrayed in our culture. My definition of what it meant to be a strong woman was shaped by my mother and her history. I defined myself as a feminist because she was the role model who drove me to pursue the career of my choice, and to speak out if I ever felt cheated or judged unfairly.

Now that my daughter is of the age where she's facing important decisions about her future, the question of what it means to be a feminist in the twenty-first century—more than fifty years after *The Feminine Mystique*—has come into sharp focus. Even from the time I started working on this book, the cultural debate about the definition of feminism has heated up on op-ed pages, in academia, and in pop culture. For female celebrities, the question "Are you a feminist?" has become a "gotcha" moment in media interviews. It's disconcerting to see prominent stars disavow the F-word because they associate it with disliking men and all the other negative connotations heaped on the term by those who fear true gender equality.

Sheryl Sandberg, chief operating officer of Facebook, helped spark this conversation with her powerful message about the importance of encouraging women to step up as leaders in her 2013 book, *Lean In: Women, Work, and the Will to Lead*. Since then a number of commentators have weighed in with articles and essays attempting to answer some of my questions: Why does it seem that the modern women's movement has stalled? What do we need to do—what should we do—to revive a spirit of activism and advocacy without excuses, without apologies or without qualifications?

It was invigorating to see no less a superstar than Beyoncé taking a stand on the F-word and send a powerful message to young people by performing at MTV's 2014 Video Music Awards against a backdrop of "FEMINIST" in giant block letters. Actress Emma Watson made headlines—and drew a standing ovation—with her impassioned and articulate twelve-minute speech declaring herself a feminist at the United Nations in September 2014. She spoke in her capacity as a UN

Women Goodwill Ambassador and unveiled the launch of the HeForShe campaign to enlist men and boys to work toward ending gender inequality in all its forms.

"The more I've spoken about feminism, the more I have realized that fighting for women's rights has too often become synonymous with man-hating," Watson said. "If there is one thing I know for certain it is that this has to stop."

After all the gains of the past hundred years, how can we possibly still live in a world where women still account for less than 5 percent of the CEO posts in Fortune 500 companies? How is it possible that a national retailer could market a T-shirt for girls that proclaimed: "I'm too pretty to do my math homework so my brother has to do it for me"? Somebody at JCPenney thought that was a good idea. In 2011.

Oscar-winning actress Geena Davis, a friend of mine from our college days at Boston University, was so dismayed at the portrayals of female characters in children's media after she had her daughter that she launched the Institute on Gender in Media. She funded it out of her own pocket at the start in an effort to generate credible academic research on how gender images in media affect all of our children. One of the most surprising facts uncovered by the research her institute has funded is the documentation that male characters outnumber females three-to-one in family- and kid-friendly films—a ratio that hasn't changed since the 1940s. Geena writes with humor in her essay for this collection about the experiences with her daughter, Alizeh, that led her to establish the institute and its advocacy arm, See Jane.

My own principles of striving to be open-minded and respectful of individual choice have been tested by the growth in the number of highly educated, highly skilled women who "opt out" of the labor force to focus on raising children. Some have argued that this is a new form of feminism—the ability to disengage from working outside the home if that's where your passion lies.

The renewed scrutiny of the social status of women sparked by *Lean In* has shed light on the reality that while we may have lost the sense of being part of a broad-based national "movement" to press for equal rights, there are many more platforms out there for women to make their voices heard—no matter what they choose to express. Unfortunately, the increasing tendency by the media to divide mothers into categories has a negative effect in making both women and men more judgmental of the parenting and lifestyle choices that we make. Why can't we all just be moms?

It's easy to get discouraged—until you see people like Ms. Watson claiming the mantle for the next generation. The movement is there, but it's more diffuse and diverse than in the early days of *Ms. Magazine*. It's analogous to the fundamental changes I've seen across the television business, which has evolved from a marketplace dominated by three networks (CBS, NBC, and ABC) to a universe of 200-plus channels and a multitude of screens in the typical American home. Ideas of what it means to be a feminist are as plentiful as new television shows these days.

I embrace the diversity of this modern patchwork quilt. We have come a long way but we have miles to go. The mothering instinct makes us want to equip our daughters and our sons with everything they need to be happy, healthy, successful, and fulfilled.

In *The Feminine Mystique,* Betty Friedan famously asserted that "the personal is political" for women in defining who they are and what they are able to achieve. It doesn't get any more personal than the shared experiences of mothers and daughters. In these pages I hope readers will find inspiration, insights, and ideas for the most meaningful ways to impart the values and the beliefs that we prize the most as modern mothers. It's never too early, or too late, to start packing that backpack.

WHAT I TOLD
MY DAUGHTER

Through My Daughter's Eyes

GEENA DAVIS

Actress-advocate

When my daughter, Alizeh, was about five years old, I had a life-changing revelation while watching a video of the Disney film *Mulan* with her.

But my epiphany wasn't what you might guess: that I was thrilled for her to see a female lead character who was a strong and brave (and funny!) leader. After all, this was a story about a young woman who ultimately saves all of China! And I adored it for that. No, this revelation was not brought about by the movie but by something my daughter asked while watching. It was the scene where the other soldiers find out that Mulan is actually a girl and throw her out of the army. Alizeh looked up at me with a deeply wounded expression and asked in a voice filled with emotion, "Why *can't* girls be in the army?"

I suddenly realized the implication of what she was asking,

and it hit me like a punch to the stomach: she had no idea that there was inequality between the genders. She hadn't an inkling, yet, that there were some things that were considered unsuitable for girls—some things that girls were seen as not strong, smart, or talented enough to do. She was asking about one particular character from a certain time in history, and of course I explained that in China, at that time, girls were not allowed to be in the army. I explained that girls are very strong and capable, and that now, women are very important members of the military.

But the question contained a world of heartache for me: This soulful little girl, whom I had so carefully encouraged to believe she could do anything, would come to learn that not everyone thinks that way. I'd protected her from Cinderella thus far, but I couldn't ultimately protect her from discovering that untold millions of girls and women throughout millennia had learned the same thing too, sometimes through neglect, misery, or abuse.

I realized, in that moment, that she would inevitably absorb the message that girls and women are less important to the world than men and boys. And I fully took in the tragedy of that happening, to her and to all girls.

One of the most disturbing aspects was that the message would largely be taken in unconsciously; she would see things that are meant to train her not to notice gender imbalance, to expect an uneven playing field, to lower her expectations. She would see countless print images, TV shows, movies, video games, and by the time she was eighteen, half a million commercials telling her how she is supposed to look.

Over the decade prior to our viewing of *Mulan*, I'd hap-

pened to play some very cool characters: a baseball phenome-
non, a newly minted road warrior . . . even a female amnesiac
assassin. Through these roles, I became keenly aware of the
way women are depicted in the entertainment industry—or
not depicted, considering how few female characters there
actually are. I realized that women in the audience rarely get
to see exciting and inspiring female characters. I resolved that,
whenever possible, I would choose roles that women might
find empowering.

But as I watched more children's media through my daughter's eyes, I was floored to see that our youngest boys and girls
are seeing and absorbing the same imbalanced view of the
world that our culture peddles to the rest of us. Kids' media
is training children from the very beginning to see male characters doing most of the interesting things, and to see gender
imbalance as the norm. As a mother, I thought that surely kids
should be seeing boys and girls sharing the sandbox equally in
the twenty-first century.

I took this observation seriously. So seriously that I launched
a nonprofit research organization several years ago, the Geena
Davis Institute on Gender in Media. We've now sponsored
the largest amount of research ever done on gender depictions
in media aimed at children, covering a twenty-year span. The
results confirmed my worst fears.

In family-rated movies and children's television, for every
female speaking character there are three male characters. If
you look specifically at crowd scenes in films, the percentage of
female characters goes down to 17 percent, in both animated
and live-action movies. You'd think you'd almost have to go out
of your way to leave out that many female characters! We also

looked at the quality of the characters, not just the quantity: for example, our comprehensive research on characters' occupations in family films showed that 81 percent of the jobs were held by men; one of the most common functions of a female character was to serve as "eye candy." Topping it all off, there was no increase in the percentage of female characters over the twenty-year span.

So what message are we sending girls and boys? If the female characters are one-dimensional, sidelined, stereotyped, or simply not there at all, we're saying that women and girls are less valuable to our society than men and boys. That women and girls don't take up half the space in the world.

And the message is sinking in: the more hours of TV a girl watches, the more limited she thinks her options are in life; the more boys watch, the more sexist their views become.

By feeding our youngest kids a seriously imbalanced world from the beginning, we are in effect training yet another generation to view gender imbalance as the norm. This happened to all of us—it doesn't matter when you grew up, you saw exactly the same imbalance in entertainment media: the ratio of male to female characters in movies has been exactly the same since 1946.

I can't stop our culture from sending disempowering messages to my daughter, no matter how much I limit her media exposure. But I can tell her that it's wrong. I can teach her that it's unfair and needs to change. I can't stop people from complimenting me on her appearance as if she's just an object. But I can tell her later why that's inappropriate. Maybe no woman has been president of the United States yet, but her mother has—on TV! I can tell her how to form her own opinions and not let our culture dictate what's appropriate for women to be and do.

And I do tell her. Alizeh and her twin brothers have limited exposure to TV and movies, but when they do watch, I am usually right there with them, so I can point out the inequities and misrepresentations; I tell them how to be savvy media consumers. But now, at eleven years old, Alizeh is telling me things. Before I can even lean in to whisper an observation, she will turn to me and say, "Mom, look. There aren't enough girls."

———

Geena Davis is an Academy Award–winning actress and founder of the Geena Davis Institute on Gender in Media.

Future Women Presidents

CECILE RICHARDS

Nonprofit executive

I come from a long line of strong women. My daughter is one of them.

Growing up, our family was a bit of a matriarchy. My father's mother, born at the turn of the century, was ahead of her time in pushing for civil rights, and she helped start the League of Women Voters in Waco, Texas. My other grandmother was so tough that legend has it she wrung a chicken's neck from the birthing bed while in labor with my mom, just to make sure that my granddad had something for supper. Of course, the state of Texas was civilized by women who could hunt, split logs, and live on the frontier. They built schools and communities. They were "doing it all" long before it was a topic of daytime TV, and my grandmothers were of that mold.

My mom, Ann Richards, was no slouch in the strong

woman department. She moved from being a 1950s house-wife to governor of Texas. Even after her passing in 2006, she continues to be the center of the family solar system in many ways.

With this background, I had plenty of inspiring role models in my youth. But I was in for a shock when I began the journey of raising two daughters and a son. I quickly realized that the world outside wasn't as feminist-friendly as our family.

By the time the kids were tall enough to reach the candy in the checkout line at the grocery store, I realized that star-ing them in the face were women's magazines portraying a bizarre idea of what women grew up to be: fashion-crazed and men-obsessed supermodels. Where were the cover photos of women athletes and astronauts?

But it was only after my twins, Daniel and Hannah, started school that I realized how early their expectations about life were established. Their wonderful teacher handed out awards at the end of the year. The boys got prizes such as "most likely to invent something" or "most inquisitive," while the girls got "most helpful in class." I wanted Hannah to get "most likely to rule the world." I was determined that my daughters would grow up to be self-confident and fearless, along with my son.

As elementary school went on, it seemed like the confidence-building opportunities for Hannah were few. So along with some other moms and our daughters, we created our own group—one where we wouldn't have to sell anything or wear uniforms. We asked the girls to name it, and they de-cided to call themselves the "Future Women Presidents." They designed their own T-shirts and proudly wore them wherever we went.

Over the next few years, we had great adventures. We toured the White House and practiced at the Press Club lectern. We camped in the Shenandoah Mountains and learned to start a fire and cook outside. We visited the women's history museum and learned about Mexican artist Frida Kahlo and other adventurous women. We designed a mural and volunteered for community service. We didn't have a pinewood derby to compete in, but we did the kinds of cool things that the boys were doing.

As Hannah grew up and out of the Future Women Presidents, she took on the toughest assignment imaginable: pitching for her softball team in junior high school.

A terrific softball player, Hannah's favorite position was shortstop—a challenging role, and one that avoided the spotlight of the pitcher's mound. But every team needs a pitcher, and someone had to step up—so Hannah volunteered, along with three of her teammates. That meant putting in hours of extra training on the weekends, developing the strategy and technique to be a pitcher. One by one, the others quit, until Hannah was the last player standing.

Learning to pitch turned out to be the easy part. More challenging was learning to rise to the occasion when the team, the coach, and all of the fans and families on the sidelines were counting on Hannah to perform under pressure. As she stood on that mound pitching through some tough innings, I watched Hannah learn how to handle that pressure with grace—fiercely determined to win, but never embarrassed to lose as long as she had left it all on the field. There was one memorable weekend that summed up Hannah in a nutshell: On Saturday, Hannah didn't pitch particularly well, and her team lost to their archrivals. The next day, undeterred, she volunteered to pitch again. Her infectious determination led not only to one of her best games, but lifted the spirit and confidence of her teammates.

Pitching was her first real leadership role, and Hannah learned an important lesson about going back out on the field, even when her team was losing or morale was down. Those lonely moments on the mound helped her find and develop her willingness to take on challenges going forward. As she worked through high school and then college, she threw herself into campus organizing and later community organizing with the confidence worthy of a Future Women Presidents alumna.

The good news is that all three of my kids ended up being strong feminists, including Hannah's twin brother. Daniel became the vice president of the reproductive rights group on his college campus, and fought to get birth control access at the college health center. And my elder daughter, Lily, can remember every lesson her governor grandmother ever taught her. Today she is following that advice with a vengeance. Mom's most important piece of wisdom? Remember that this is the only life we get and do it now—no look-backs, no do-overs.

I'm grateful that my kids are now part of the most diverse, most progressive generation ever in this country. They are passionate and committed to social justice. They are fighters for LGBT rights and immigrant rights and environmental justice. They all give me hope for our future. And I'm confident that one day, they will help elect a future woman president.

Cecile Richards is president of the Planned Parenthood Federation of America and the Planned Parenthood Action Fund. Under her leadership, Planned Parenthood has expanded its advocacy for women's health care and reproductive rights. Before joining Planned Parenthood in 2006, she was deputy chief of staff to US Representative Nancy Pelosi. Earlier in her career she was a labor organizer.

Sacrifices

DOLORES HUERTA

Labor leader—community organizer

I was a young mother when I first became involved in community organizing, which set me on the path to lead a labor movement as cofounder with Cesar Chavez of the United Farm Workers union.

While we worked day and night to improve the lives of farmworkers, I had another nearly full-time job in trying to recruit people to help watch my children. Over the course of three marriages, I had eleven kids—seven daughters and four sons.

If I needed to go to a meeting or attend a demonstration or a recruiting effort, it was always a juggling act to find friends and family members that I could count on to take care of my kids when I needed to be away. When I think about my forty years with the UFW, I can't help but think about how many times I had to scramble to arrange child care.

My children grew up on the front lines of a historic movement. They were at my side during protest marches, on picket
lines, and at meetings that made a huge difference in the lives
of workers, particularly Latino immigrants. I have always been
passionate about working to make the world a better place for
the less fortunate. My children made sacrifices during their
youth so that I could devote so much of my time to this cause.
To this day, I still feel guilty about it.

My children didn't have the same luxuries that I enjoyed as a
kid. I grew up in a middle-class household in Stockton, California. My mother took me to the ballet and to concerts with great
musicians such as Jascha Heifetz. I had music lessons, dance
lessons, and a very stable home life. I was a Girl Scout in good
standing until I was eighteen. My children had none of that.

Growing up with a labor organizer for a mother, they had
experiences you can't buy, and they met great people. But I still
feel bad sometimes that they didn't have a more traditional upbringing. They were always on the move with me, or we were
apart for long stretches. It wasn't easy for any of us.

I first became an activist in 1955 when I had two young
daughters, Celeste and Lori. I decided to join the Stockton
Community Service Organization. After graduating high
school, I'd worked as a teacher, and I was tired of seeing kids in
my classes suffering from poverty and hunger. My husband and
I divorced not long after, and I threw myself into organizing the
local Agricultural Workers Association to help the community
of fieldworkers.

Chavez was executive director of the CSO. We hit it off
immediately. We shared a vision of the need for a farmworkers'
union, not just a service organization. We resigned from the

CSO in 1962 and moved to Delano, California, to begin our organizing campaign. Delano is in California's Central Valley, an agricultural area about 150 miles north of Los Angeles where farmworkers faced deplorable working conditions. The more I saw, the more passionate I became about helping farmworkers.

By this time I'd had five more children with my second husband. The work with Chavez and the UFW was so intense that I left some of my younger kids in Stockton with family members. My husband's family was not happy with this. They wanted me to be a more traditional wife and mother.

But my mother taught me a few important lessons while I was growing up. One was to always be yourself, and don't try to pretend to be somebody different. Another was to never be afraid to try new things. And she also instilled in me and my brothers a strong desire to help other people and try to make the world a better place.

My mother, Alicia St. John Chavez, was a businesswoman who had a big heart. She ran her own restaurant in Stockton, and she became friends with a Japanese woman in town who ran a hotel. During World War II, when Japanese Americans were sent to internment camps in the United States, my mother's friend asked her to take over the hotel.

My mother ran the seventy-room hotel and kept the business in good shape, even as she often opened the doors to farmworkers and others who couldn't afford to pay for rooms. After the war, when the owner of the hotel property refused to let the Japanese family renew their lease, my mother helped them start new businesses. They remained lifelong friends.

My mother's example stands out when I think of how important women were to the success of the UFW and in the community-organizing work that I've done since 2002 with the Dolores Huerta Foundation.

Women do the majority of the heavy lifting in our social-justice campaigns. We fight for everything from building neighborhood swimming pools and parks to improving sewage systems to establishing teen pregnancy prevention programs. Women get very enthusiastic when we help give them the tools they need to effect change. It's amazing how much they can accomplish even when they have to work and take care of their own families. Sometimes they have to battle their husbands to let them become active. I remember one woman was getting a hard time from her husband about being a member of a UFW committee and going to meetings at night. We told him that it was part of a new law signed by the governor of California, and that she had to participate. He bought it.

My children saw this kind of human drama play out in front of them almost every day. They may have lacked some comforts, but they were well prepared to take on the world by the time they reached adulthood. I'm proud to say that they are all active in public service in one way or another.

One of my sons put himself through medical school by cleaning bathrooms at night. Another son had a catering business that helped feed poor kids in ghetto neighborhoods. One of my daughters helped launch a center for LGBT teens at her high school to provide a place where kids could get counseling and support.

My daughters tell me they loved it when I would tell them that they could be whatever they wanted to be in life, and that they should never be afraid to try new things. I pretty much passed on the values my mother taught me. Like my mother, I tried to be a role model in demonstrating my commitment to my work. I know I've helped make the world a better place with the UFW and with my foundation, and my children helped me do it. To me, this reflects the true spirit of the UFW motto *Si se puede*. Yes we can.

———————

Dolores Huerta has spent more than fifty years as a labor organizer and community activist. She cofounded the United Farm Workers union with Cesar Chavez in 1962. Since 2002, she has headed the Dolores Huerta Foundation in Bakersfield, California. Among her many accolades, Huerta received the Presidential Medal of Freedom in 2012, and she was inducted into the California Hall of Fame in 2013.

Dear Eva

RABBI SHARON BROUS

Dear Eva,

You were so sad when I left for Africa. I want to share with you why I went, what I learned, and what I dream for you, your brother and sister. I don't expect that you'll understand all of this right now, but I hope that you'll look back one day when you're bigger and it will make more sense.

When you were born, Aunt Paulette told me that having a child is like wearing your heart outside your chest. You realize pretty quickly as a parent that the thing you love most in the world is something you can't fully protect, no matter what. It's a kind of vulnerability that's almost too much to bear. And it's something I have thought about every day since your birth.

Someone called me recently after dropping his daughter off at college in New York. "Rabbi, I finally understand why you always talk about tikkun olam," he said. "Try to make the world more just because one day you'll let go of someone you love deeply, and all you can do is hope and pray that the world is decent, kind, and fair."

It's important, Eva, that you know that one nearly universal thread, across ethnic, cultural, and geographical boundaries, is the oppression of girls and women. Women in poor communities throughout the developing world have it the worst. They often have no access to basic medical services and far too many die in childbirth. In most of the world, girls are the last ones to get food when there's not enough for everyone to eat. And when desperate families can't afford to send their kids to school, only the boys get to learn. Girls, even very little girls, are sent out to beg or find work—and when they go, people often hurt and take advantage of them in unthinkable ways. When war comes, women's and girls' bodies are treated like a battlefield as soldiers try to break their enemies by breaking their women. The more I have learned about the struggles of girls and women over the years, the more I began to wonder— what kind of legal action and spiritual strength would it take to change course?

That's a big part of why I went to Liberia—to meet women who had lost their children and their parents, who were stripped of their dignity and their voices, but who somehow found the strength to stand up and say, "No More!"

I met many extraordinary women on this trip, including Leymah, just a couple of years older than me. In 2002, after a decade of civil war, Leymah found herself with four hungry children to feed, no home, and no hope. Her country and her life had been shattered by war, and the fighting persisted all around her. One night in a dream, a voice told Leymah to gather the women and pray for peace. She awoke driven by a mysterious sense of purpose. Like the women of Montgomery, Alabama, after Rosa Parks's arrest, she posted signs all around the capital city of Monrovia calling for the women to meet the next morning to protest the violence and terror. At the break of dawn, Leymah stood alone in the meeting place and wondering if she had gone mad. What would she do if nobody showed up? But then, to her shock and amazement, thousands of women began approaching from all corners of the city, chanting one simple message: "We want peace. No more war!"

The warlords and government forces in Liberia were known for their brutality—they could easily have killed every last one of the protesters. I don't know where the women found their courage. Maybe they had suffered so profoundly that they felt they had nothing left to lose. As one woman told us: "We were not afraid. Either we will die from war, or we will die fighting to make peace." Maybe they found their strength together—as sisters—when they shared stories about all of the horrors that had been done to their bodies and to their loved ones. Maybe they felt the presence of God within them, realizing, like the Israelites chased by Pharaoh's chariots to the edge of the sea, that human beings deserve to be free. That God stands with the righteous. And that we must be brave and walk toward our own liberation, even against impossible odds.

Thousands of women returned day after day for a year—in the blazing sun and pouring rain, refusing to move until the men made peace. In white T-shirts and scarves, they stared down generals, warlords, and soldiers. Leymah, like Queen Esther before her, gathered all of her strength and cried out before the president:

The women of Liberia are tired of war. We are tired of running. We are tired of begging . . . We are tired of our children being raped. We are now taking this stand to secure the future of our children. Because we believe, as custodians of our society, that tomorrow our children will ask us, "Mama, what was your role during the crisis?"

Believe it or not, the women won. The president was forced to step down and the rebels (about 40,000 of them) turned in their guns and grenades. In the first free election right after the war, a woman named Ellen Johnson Sirleaf was chosen to be the new president of Liberia. A woman president! She may have the hardest job in the world—helping an impoverished and traumatized country heal and rebuild—but the very fact of her presidency gives hope that change is truly possible.

Eva, I know this is a hard story to hear. The suffering in our world is real, and nothing will ever change if we remain detached from other people and indifferent to their struggles.

I hope you understand why I needed to meet Leymah and her sisters in person. I wanted to hear their stories, to hold their hands and pray with them. I wanted to thank them for reminding us what real moral courage looks like, and for showing the world how much strength women have when we stand together. I wanted to bring home their protest T-shirts so that when you and your sister feel like you need some extra strength you can put one on and feel the power of sisterhood, even over time and overseas. And I felt that I had to let these women know that they were not alone. This is so important, Eva, because when armies have come after our people, too often the rest of the world has pretended that it was not their problem. I don't ever want someone else to feel as alone and invisible as we have felt in our own darkest hour.

Eva, I often wonder who you'll be when you grow up. I hope you'll fall in love. I hope you'll get to be a mother—to feel the indescribable blessing of holding a tiny creature in your arms and watching her grow into herself, discover her voice, love, defy, love more. I hope you'll find wisdom and hope in Torah and the traditions of our people. I pray that your sweet heart will be able to hold the pain and the heartache and the breathtaking beauty and majesty of our world all at once. I pray that you'll find a way to use the gifts God has given you to help turn the dial toward justice and compassion, healing and possibility. And I hope you'll always know that I love you with all my heart and being your mother is the greatest privilege of my life.

Love,
Ima

Rabbi Sharon Brous is founder of IKAR, a vibrant Jewish community in Los Angeles.

The Perfect Paradox

PEGGY ORENSTEIN

Author-advocate

My daughter sat at her desk absorbed in sketching the latest in an endless procession of manga-eyed girls. Every girl had glittery eyes, long straight hair, a tiny waist. Perfect.

She glanced up at me and smiled. "What is it, Mom?" she asked.

What indeed?

I had just read a newspaper article about Rehtaeh Parsons, the latest of a string of girls who were sexually assaulted at a party by boys, who then posted evidence of their actions on the Internet. A few months earlier, a sixteen-year-old honor student in Steubenville, Ohio, has been carted, naked and unconscious, from party to party by two young men; they penetrated her, urinated on her, and posted tweets such as, "The song of the night is definitely 'Rape Me,' by Nirvana."

There was also Savannah Dietrich, a Kentucky girl similarly assaulted by photo-snapping boys. A judge sentenced them to community service for their crime, assisting their lacrosse coach and picking up litter on their private school campus. When, outraged by the token punishment, Savannah tweeted their real names, she was threatened with a contempt of court charge for violating confidentiality.

And there was Audrie Pott, who lived not fifty miles from where I sit now. A soccer player with thick hair and a heart-shaped face, she also drank too much at a high school party. When she woke up the next morning, her shorts were off; someone had doodled pictures and slurs all over her body with a Sharpie. On one leg, a boy had signed his name, followed by the words "was here." Eight days after photos of her allegedly being assaulted were posted on the Internet, she hanged herself.

These tragedies bring up so many issues: teenage alcohol abuse; boys' treatment of girls; girls' lack of support for one another; the impact of social media on kids. But something else struck me, too, as I read these stories: the victims' reluctance to confide what had happened to an adult. What kept them silent—even to the point of self-harm—in the face of violation? Were there other, more mundane ways girls believed they can't rely on our trust or support?

My baby was only nine; she didn't fully understand what sex was, let alone rape, and it was not something I was eager to explain. So I paused at her doorway, wondering what it was I wanted to say.

"So," I began. "I was just reading about a girl who was bullied and blamed herself."

My daughter nodded. "I heard sometimes kids kill themselves when that happens."

I caught my breath. She knew about suicide? What else had my fourth grader heard?

"That's true," I said, more calmly than I felt. "And I think that's partly because they feel alone. They don't want to tell their parents what's happening because they think their parents will be disappointed in them. And I don't want you to worry about that. Daddy and I want you to make good decisions with friends and at school. We know you do make good decisions. But sometimes you might not. You might actually make a bad decision. You might make a really bad decision or do something we've told you not to do and something might happen that you didn't intend. And even then, you can tell us."

"Okay," she said, and turned back to her drawing.

I wondered if it was. One awkwardly blurted lecture would obviously not do the trick, but even if it didn't sink in with her it got me thinking. Parents I know, moms especially, tell our girls that they can do anything, be anything, that the world is theirs for the taking. We encourage them—expect them—to be ultrahigh achievers with lofty goals for college and beyond. We bask in the successes of this new, unstoppable generation. There is nothing wrong with that. I want my daughter to be self-sufficient. I want her to be compassionate. I want her to feel no limits to her potential in the classroom or the workplace. I want her sexuality to develop as a source of pleasure and intimacy.

Yet, I fear we may sometimes put too much pressure on our girls, imbue them with impossible standards. I worry that our dreams for them may sometimes, unintentionally, lead them to believe they can never make mistakes, they can disappoint us—that we are teaching them, to their peril, that perfection is more important than resilience. Researchers at Duke University, for instance, have found that female students believe they must be effortlessly "smart, accomplished, fit, beautiful, and popular." When they fell short—whether they gained a pound or got an A– on a test or were sexually assaulted at a party— their shame, culpability, and sense of personal failure was both total and secret: they kept the façade, but turned the feelings inward, against themselves, compromising their mental health and well-being.

Truth? I do believe my daughter is perfect. I have thought she was perfect since the day she was born. Yet, I know her life won't be, can't be. She will fail. She will know pain. She might be bullied in school or online or in some future cyborgish way that I can't even imagine. If she thinks she needs to be "perfect" she will never make it through. So I want her to know not only that she can succeed, but that she can fail without being a failure, be hurt without being diminished, be embarrassed without being shamed. I want her to know that she has both internal resources and external ones, that she does not want or need to be that manga-eyed, perfect girl, that sometimes life is not effortless, it's not effortless at all. And I want her to know, mostly, that if things get hard—when they get hard—she is not alone: her dad and I will always, always, always be there to love her, to catch her, to stand by her, and, when she needs it, to help her stand back up.

———

Peggy Orenstein is the bestselling author of *Cinderella Ate My Daughter: Dispatches from the Frontlines of the New Girlie-Girl Culture*, and other books. She is a contributor to the *New York Times Magazine*, NPR, and other media outlets and is a frequent speaker and media commentator.

The Danger of Fear

DEBORA BLACK

Police chief

When God blessed me with a baby girl, I felt a joy so overwhelming I thought my heart would burst. But this was followed by a strong feeling of anxiety. How would I keep my precious daughter safe from all the threats and dangers in our world?

As a police officer, protecting people is what I do—it's in my DNA. I was working for the Phoenix Police Department when Mallory was born in 1991. My career in law enforcement has led me to become the first female police chief in Glendale, Arizona, and one of the few women in the country to lead a police department in a sizable city. But for all my experience on the force, my daughter still taught me important lessons in managing the debilitating effects of fear that made me a more effective public servant.

The alignment of my role as a mom and my hardwired need to protect was complicated, to say the least. The basics were simple: the car safety seat, vaccinations, sunscreen, bike helmet, cross at the light, and "don't talk to strangers"—those are rules that are rooted in common sense and easy to follow. This was not what kept me up at night. I was troubled by the danger I knew far too much about but felt powerless to control, even with my badge. I knew from experience that bad things happen to good people every day, and lessons about stranger danger felt insufficient to safeguard my daughter from predators, violent criminals, and even terrorists.

Mallory relished my work as a police officer even though it was an uncommon job for a mom to have. When I showed up for career day at her school in a squad car, she thought it was cool, and her friends agreed. When I taught her Girl Scout troop the phonetic alphabet codes that officers use to communicate ("One-Adam-12," etc.) and the Heimlich maneuver, she paid attention.

She was learning important lessons even during those times when she was forced to wait not so patiently for me to finish work at the station. She witnessed the amazing bond that exists among people in law enforcement. By extension, it became her second family, and infused the value of everyone looking out for one another.

My daughter was five when a bomb leveled the Alfred P. Murrah Federal Building in downtown Oklahoma City. She was just nine on September 11, 2001. In the wake of September 11, many predicted that children old enough to have an awareness of the attack on the World Trade Center would be haunted by the memory and grow up apprehensive and mistrustful. I watched for those signs in my daughter while barely acknowledging how much I myself had changed. I viewed the world through a lens of fear and hesitation, not for myself or as a police officer, but because I worried about the vulnerability of my child. I was concerned about the things outside my control, and I worried about doing enough to manage the risks I could control. These are not good qualities for a law enforcement professional or for a mother.

In time, as my world shrunk under the weight of this pointless worry, I realized my daughter was thriving. By the grace of God, she embraced the positive things I demonstrated to her about courage, faith, and doing the right thing. She rejected the unproductive aspects of worry, and instead internalized the essential lessons of recognizing true fear and knowing what actions to take when faced with a real threat. She possessed the wonderful gifts of discernment and healthy caution as she set the course of her life.

My daughter had her passport before she had a driver's license. She has traveled the world to work in poverty-stricken areas on mission trips. At nineteen, she set out to live on her own in a neighboring city—with no consideration of crime rate. Today, she lives and owns a business in Seattle and couldn't be happier. She is a fiercely independent and confident young woman who accepts people without judgment and revels in the magnificence of life. And she is safe.

Mallory tells me that I taught her the meaning of courage every day that I stepped out of the house in uniform. Even as I fought my own worries, Mallory learned the importance of responding decisively to real danger, but not allowing fear to stop you from experiencing all that life has to offer.

The principles that I know so well as a police chief were things I had to learn as a mother. Protecting our children from things that may realistically harm them is our fundamental responsibility as adults. But if we burden our kids with artificial worry about things neither they nor we can control, we steal their joy today and limit the promise of their tomorrow.

Debora Black has been the chief of police in Glendale, Arizona, since 2011. Before Glendale, she served more than twenty-five years with the Phoenix Police Department, starting her career in law enforcement as a patrol officer in 1980. Black was awarded the Medal of Valor, three Medals of Lifesaving, and two police chief's Unit Awards during her tenure in Phoenix.

Be Nice to the Fat Girls

AYELET WALDMAN

Author

Laid side by side, Sophie is six inches shorter than her duffel bag, and yet this child is going off to sleepaway camp. Six years old, with the uncanny confidence of a grown woman, she has packed her bags herself, rejecting the pile of pink frills that only the year before were all she would consider wearing, in favor of utilitarian T-shirts and shorts. Her cascade of curls is shoved back behind her ears and she's so excited she's dancing rather than standing. At this age, I, too, was sent off to summer camp, but I went nervously, so small and anxious that the two months seemed more like two years. Sophie is going only for a week, as much as I could contemplate, and less than she wanted. She is, this sturdy creature, everything that I wasn't. She is tall and assured, immune to anxiety and self-doubt. She is the kind of child who touches a harp for the first time and announces, with ludicrous confidence, "I am a very good harpist."

My daughter makes friends easily, and this more than anything else confuses me about her. Throughout my early years my parents moved so frequently that I was almost always the new girl, the odd girl. By the time they set down roots, I had become a strange little girl, smaller and younger than my classmates, a weird girl who read a lot and alternated between expressing loud opinions and cowering before the impenetrable web of childhood social interactions. But not Sophie. At six, she towers above most of the other girls, and revels in her powerful role in the social network. I knew exactly how to be a good mother to the outcast child. I have no idea what to make of this Queen Bee.

Without a backward glance, Sophie climbs onto the big yellow bus that will take her away from home for the first time. I watch her settle herself in a seat. The bus gears grind, it belches smoke, and then they are off. Before I even know that I am doing it, I am running alongside the bus, my hands a megaphone around my lips, shouting.

"Be nice to the fat girls!" I holler. "Be kind to the lonely girls! Be generous!"

Though by now all I see in the bus window is my own reflection, I know, because we are still connected, my girl and I, through a phantom umbilicus that will never be entirely severed, that she is rolling her eyes.

Fast-forward a decade, and Sophie has unsurprisingly turned into a tall, confident, self-assured young woman. It is her senior year of high school, and if she is no longer the Queen Bee, that is because she herself has rejected that role. She chooses her friends carefully, values the company of a few intimates over the horde. It comes to her attention somehow, through the vagaries of teen social media, I suppose, that a group of popular male athletes in her class have started a "dogfight," a competition in which the loser must ask out on a date a girl whom they've decided is ugly, beneath the contempt of their glorious, shiny jock selves. Sophie is furious, and, along with a small group of her girlfriends, goes to the administration, demanding justice on behalf of this girl and of all girls subject to this environment. This action is not without a cost. Those boys are beloved, they are the reigning royalty of the school, who will ride the tide of their privilege, good looks, and athletic ability all the way to the Ivy League. But my girl gives no thought to the social price she will pay, and storms on.

A few months later, unpunished, these very boys take to the stage in an all-school community meeting to rap about "bitches" and "hos," and my daughter returns to the office of the head of the school. She describes what it feels like to be a girl in that auditorium and in that school. She uses words like "sexism" and phrases like "rape culture," and my chest is nearly bursting with pride. When the head expresses his hope that her experience at the school has not been unduly tainted by this episode and others like it, she frowns at him, confused.

"It's not about me," she explains. "I'm fine." And she is, and always was, fine. More than fine. "It's about the girls who come after me. The juniors, sophomores, and most of all the freshmen, who don't have the confidence to stand up for themselves, and who are learning that being a woman means tolerating this kind of abuse."

When I told Sophie I was asked to write an essay about the

most important lesson I'd taught her, she immediately replied, "Be nice to the fat girls." And the lonely, and the poor, and the lost. What I tried to teach and what she learned far better than I could ever have hoped is that those of us who are privileged, who suffer no racial discrimination, who don't worry if we can afford our next meal, who are safe and secure in the world, must share the fruits of this privilege, must care for others, must always be thinking of those who have less and need more. I had dreamed of nurturing a confident, generous woman, but in the end Sophie invented herself, and what she has become has exceeded my wildest and most hopeful imaginings. She is a warrior. And though it was not I who made this marvel, I realize that perhaps, in some ways, I was precisely the mother she needed to become the person she was meant to be.

———————

Ayelet Waldman is a novelist and author of the *New York Times* bestseller *Bad Mother: A Chronicle of Maternal Crimes, Minor Calamities and Occasional Moments of Grace.* Her other books include *Love and Treasure, Red Hook Road,* and *Love and Other Impossible Pursuits.* Her work has appeared in the *New York Times, Wall Street Journal, Washington Post,* and *Vogue.* On radio, she has been a contributor to *This American Life* and *All Things Considered.*

The Estrogen Express

PAT BENATAR

Singer-songwriter

Raising kids is a lot like the old slogan for the Peace Corps: It's the toughest job you'll ever love.

It was tough for my husband, Neil "Spyder" Giraldo, and I to raise our daughters and maintain our careers in the rock 'n' roll business. Spyder is not only my soul mate, he's also my No. 1 musical collaborator and producer. Once we were blessed with two beautiful girls, we decided there was no way we were going to miss their childhood.

As soon as Haley and Hana were old enough to go to school, we only toured during the summer so they could come with us on the road. Strollers, playpens, toys, and bicycles were all packed onto a bus, and our band and crew members were on notice to act appropriately.

My daughters grew up like gypsies, with formative moments

like first steps and first swims coming at hotels and concert venues rather than at our home. We once had all of our musicians and crew members dress up in costume so we could give our four-year-old the experience of trick-or-treating—in the corridors of our hotel. In the hours leading up to our shows, the girls could usually be found riding their bikes like crazy up and down the aisles of an empty concert venue.

It was unconventional, for sure, but it was all time we spent together as a family. Spyder and I insisted on this, over the unbelievable objections of our record company. They even pressured me to hide my first pregnancy.

We couldn't have pulled it off had Spyder and I not been such close partners, committed to each other in every way. We come from very different backgrounds—he's a midwesterner, I'm from New York City—but we've been perfectly matched since the day we met in 1979.

My approach to being a wife and being a mother was shaped by my experience as the daughter of two working parents. Equality was gospel in our house. Everyone's paycheck counted and both parents had to share the duties of child-rearing and home maintenance. It wasn't uncommon to see my mother or grandmother mowing the lawn or painting the house. Everybody worked hard and was treated with equal respect.

Spyder and I found it was natural to work together because we shared the same core values. Even before we had children, we never went for the crazy rock 'n' roll lifestyle. I was afraid I'd lose my voice, let alone my life. The beautiful partnership we forged has guided how we lived our lives, raised our family, and loved each other. This is the most important example we've set for the girls. We made a promise to each other to put the girls' needs first, no matter what the cost, from the instant that little stick turned blue.

Early in my career, when I would go into the studio to record I had to make sure I had just the right mood lighting, just the right incense burning in order to lay down the perfect track. But all that changed by the time Hana was a toddler. One day we were working in our home studio, and I was concentrating so hard on my vocal. When I opened my eyes, I saw my little one's face pressed against the glass saying, "Mama." I knew it was time to go change a diaper, and then jump back in to finish off the chorus.

Plenty of nights on the road I would be breast-feeding right up until a few minutes before I had to hit the stage. You learned to be fast on your feet as a performer, so when showtime came, I tucked my boob back in and went onstage to be sexy. My record company at the time was relentless about pressuring us to tour more, and they warned me I'd better be skinny again when I emerged after having Haley. It was exhausting.

The only person I knew who could relate to my experience back then was Chrissie Hynde, the leader of The Pretenders, who had her second baby about four months before I had Haley in 1985. We ran into each other at an awards show and I asked her how she was doing. She said, "I'm not," and I knew exactly what she meant.

Thankfully, by the time I had Hana in 1994, the world had changed a lot for women in my profession. Spyder and I happily kept doing our own thing with the family. When it was time to hit the road, the girls would make themselves at home on the tour bus, decorating their bunks on the bus with posters and stickers. To them, it was like going to summer camp. For the longest time, they thought everybody's mom was a singer and that all kids spent their summers touring the country. They got to see so much, and learn so much, on our journeys. The only time our girls were left with nannies was when we were onstage—otherwise we were full-time Mom and Dad.

We had no other choice. No matter what you do, no matter your background, no matter how cool you think you are, when you see that newborn's face for the first time, a primal instinct takes over and you are forever changed. You will never put yourself first again. You will never stop worrying whether your child is happy, healthy, scared, or loved. And even when they've driven you to wonder whether it's okay to have multiple cocktails before 4 o'clock in the afternoon, you love them with every fiber of your being.

As much as we prize equality in our family, there's no denying that poor Spyder has been totally outnumbered by women. For years we've called our tour bus the Estrogen Express. Even our dogs have been female.

It takes quite a man to handle all of that energy. Haley and Hana grew up with parents whose relationship was firmly rooted in commitment, mutual respect, and adoration—values that have gotten us through life's inevitable heartbreaks and challenges.

Spyder and I have always tried to be present and to learn from our mistakes. We're focused on living our own lives, not someone else's, and we devote our energy to finding joy, not being miserable. We treat people with respect and demand it in return. We work hard to honor the gift of life we were given, and we dream incessantly. Why not?

These are the most important lessons I've shared with our daughters.

———

Pat Benatar is a four-time Grammy winner known for such enduring 1980s hits as "Hit Me With Your Best Shot," "Love Is a Battlefield," "You Better Run," and "Heartbreaker."

The Right to Choose

WHOOPI GOLDBERG
Actress

As my daughter, Alex, became a teenager, our lives changed in ways neither of us could have imagined.

After the fluke of being discovered by director Mike Nichols, suddenly I was making movies all around the country. I brought my mother out from New York to be with Alex at our home in Berkeley, California, rather than drag her out of school and on to movie sets.

Alex and I had always been close. For a long time it was just the two of us. We moved across the country from New York when she was little, first to San Diego and then to Berkeley. Each time we packed everything we had in our little Flintstones car and pedaled off on a new adventure. We never had any trouble communicating.

But after *The Color Purple*, things changed. When we were

out and about together, people would literally move her out of the way to get to me. That kind of thing has a big impact on a kid. There were times when I wasn't there for her birthday or something that was important to her. She said she understood why I was doing what I was doing, why I chose my career at that time. But she was a kid and had no real way to process it.

When Alex was fourteen, she came to me with the news that she was pregnant. I felt so many things all at once that I didn't know what to think. I was surprised because I knew that I had given Alex all the information she needed to not get pregnant. I was a child of the 1960s and '70s. I had been vocal for years in my support for a woman's right to choose when the time was right to have a baby. And when Alex told me she wanted to keep the baby, I was like, "Really? Okay. Really?"

When the shock wore off and Alex and I were able to talk again, she explained something that shook my eyes open. My daughter looked me in the eye and told me that she'd made a conscious decision that she wanted to have someone in her life to love who didn't know me. That was heavy, and hard to hear. But she told me, and I was proud of her for that.

It would have been easy enough for her to hide her pregnancy from me for a little while but she had the insight into herself to know why she wanted this baby.

But I was also freaked out. I called my mother to tell her what was happening. My mother was glad that Alex had told me first. And then she told me something about my job as a mother that I'll never forget. She had the wisdom that came from her experience as a practical nurse and a Head Start teacher.

"Believing in a woman's right to choose doesn't just mean

your choice," my mother told me. "You have to give Alex what it is she says she wants. We're here. We can help, and we can afford it."

My mother, as usual, was right. Alex's baby girl, Amara, brought joy to our lives and was born on my birthday. We got through the hardest parts together, and in our Berkeley community of actors and artists and hippies, there was no judgment. It just was what it was. Our family dynamic found a different groove. It wasn't always easy but it worked out for all of us.

When the word got out about the baby, Alex's friends were swarmed by the rags—the *National Enquirer* and the other tabloids—offering money for a picture of Amara. We were lucky to have the Gap and the brilliant photographer Annie Leibovitz come to the rescue by taking a beautiful picture of the four generations of us for an ad campaign. I will always thank the Gap for helping us find a better way to introduce Amara to the public.

Alex went back to school after she had Amara. She met a man who started out as a friend and became her husband (three times, but that's another story) and a good father to Amara and my two other grandchildren. We were lucky because so many girls in Alex's position would have been tossed out by their families; thankfully, that wasn't our family.

So, I became a grandmother at the age of thirty-four. Today, at sixty, I am a great-grandmother now that Amara, who is twenty-six (I can't believe it!)—who always told us she never wanted to have kids—has added another girl to the family. She and her husband, Chris, couldn't be happier.

I can thank my mother and my daughter for showing me

the way forward on the journey of our lives that none of us expected. Through their strength and determination, they taught me that choice means that everybody gets to make a choice— even if it's your teenage daughter and even if it's not the choice you would make. The fight we face is really a fight for every woman's right to make her own choice.

Whoopi Goldberg is an acclaimed actress, comedian, writer, and producer who is among the rare performers to have won Oscar, Emmy, Grammy, and Tony awards for her distinguished body of work. She has appeared in such notable films as *The Color Purple, Ghost, Sister Act, Sarafina!, How Stella Got Her Groove Back, The Lion King,* and *Ghosts of Mississippi.* Her television work includes *Star Trek: The Next Generation* and the "Comic Relief" philanthropic specials. On Broadway, she made her mark with the one-woman show *Whoopi Goldberg,* and has starred in *A Funny Thing Happened On the Way to the Forum,* and *Ma Rainey's Black Bottom.* She is also the first African-American woman to host the Academy Awards. Since 2007 Goldberg has served as moderator of the ABC daytime series *The View.*

Out Loud and Proud

SUSAN LOVE, MD

Surgeon—breast cancer advocate

My daughter, Katie, was raised with more awareness than most kids about the nature of sexual orientation and prejudice. In the late 1980s, my wife, Helen Cooksey, and I were on the leading edge of the "gayby" boom of gay and lesbian couples having children.

Helen and I felt we had to prepare our daughter for the possibility that she would encounter people who might have a problem with the fact that she has two moms. We wanted to make sure Katie understood that our family was just fine. If other people had an issue with us, that was their problem, not ours, and we could only feel sorry for them.

When Katie was little we talked with her about all kinds of prejudice, not just against gays and lesbians but the horrors of Nazi Germany and the courageous Americans who led the civil rights movement and the fight for women's suffrage. She got the message loud and clear.

Once after Katie had been in school for a few years, I asked her what she would say if someone asks why she has two mothers. She didn't skip a beat. "I tell them it's because they fell in love," Katie replied. As my heart swelled she added: "If they want more information I call my friend Allison over. She's a good explainer."

Helen and I were privileged to be trailblazers for gay adoption. In 1988, I gave birth to Katie, who was conceived from sperm donated by Helen's cousin. Helen and I are both surgeons, prominent in our fields, and we have lived our lives together out loud and proud. It was still unheard of back then for a gay couple to have a child.

When Katie was born, there were some eyebrows raised in our professional and social circles, and some gossiping about who the father might be. But we heralded our entry into parenthood with all the usual celebrations, including a big christening party at our home. Friends and associates came and everybody realized that there was nothing terribly exotic about us. We were like any couple overwhelmed with joy over our precious new arrival.

The importance of ensuring that Helen had full parental rights was driven home when Katie was a toddler and we joined other family members on a vacation to Mexico. At the airport in Raleigh, North Carolina, an airline official stopped us to ask if we had a letter from Katie's father allowing her to be taken out of the country. We realized then that if anything were to happen to Katie or me, Helen would have no parental rights at all.

So we set out to have Helen adopt Katie, which required a legal challenge. We won our first round, but the judge immediately sent the decision up to the appellate court. That set off a long process of scrutiny into our lives, with social workers and psychologists probing our fitness as parents, and lawyers and advocates strategizing on the best argument to defeat this blatant discrimination.

In 1993, when Katie was five, Massachusetts's Supreme Judicial Court issued a 4–3 decision in our favor. We made national headlines, and, more important, we set legal precedent far beyond Massachusetts's borders. In the years after we won our case, we'd often receive flowers at our home after a gay couple adopted a child.

All of this was part of the backdrop of Katie's childhood. Helen and I knew that to be a parent we had to be out and open about who we were in all circumstances. You can't say to your kid, "Our family is fine but don't let anybody know about us." We had to live our lives out loud, as I often say. Katie learned this lesson so well that she soon began teaching her parents about tolerance and openness.

Katie and I always had our best talks in her bedroom, in the evening when I read to her before bedtime. Once when she was about six or seven, she had something important on her mind.

"I'm worried that I might not be a lesbian," she confided.

"That's fine," I replied. "We just want you to be happy. We just care that you find somebody to share your life with who you love."

A few days later, we had a gay friend coming over for dinner—a visit that prompted more questions from Katie.

"Is he bringing his lover?"

"I don't think he has one right now."

"Well, how can he be gay?"

I explained that our friend was a man who usually fell in love with other men. As she was thinking about it I added as an aside—almost a throwaway line—that sometimes people can be attracted to both men and women. I'll never forget her response.

"Oh thank God. I think that's what I am," she said, with such relief in her voice.

In that moment I realized that I had spent so much energy making Katie understand her parents' relationship that I hadn't talked with her about different possibilities of sexual orientation. I hadn't given her the option of knowing that she didn't have to choose—that there were many ways to be happy, all of them good and acceptable. Part of being a parent is equipping your kid with the tools they need to find their own happiness. Even, in some cases, when it makes you uncomfortable.

Like the period when Katie had a brief obsession with Barbie dolls. I didn't like letting her play with them—it felt like we were endorsing every demeaning female stereotype in the world—but we did. We bought every ethnically diverse Barbie we could find. And I still couldn't stop myself from lecturing her about how Barbie doesn't represent real women.

"Real women don't have feet curved into a permanent arch, and real women don't have bodies like that or breasts like that, and real women do work and don't just change their clothes all the time," I said.

But I needn't have worried.

"I know, Mommy," Katie explained, "it's just like *101 Dalmatians*. Real dogs don't talk."

Another victory was logged when I overheard Katie planning the wedding of Barbie and Jane. Later in the day I asked her what happened with the nuptials.

"Oh. They didn't get married because Barbie had to go give a talk about breast cancer," she said, matter-of-factly.

Now that she's grown, Katie continues to teach us life lessons. Helen and I are accomplished doctors. We're very driven people. Katie is not. She is of a different generation and a different mind-set when it comes to her career. She's finding her path to happiness in her own way.

The challenge for my generation of women, LGBT and otherwise, is to understand that while we were consumed with fighting prejudice and breaking down barriers, we can't expect our kids to live the same life. Ostensibly, we fought those battles and broke those barriers so that the next generation wouldn't have to. For many of us, the hardest thing as parents is to let our grown kids just be.

My own mother would have been much happier if I had married a doctor rather than become a doctor. I had to do what I knew was right for me. The message I tried to give to my daughter was that I never wanted her to be just like me. I have only ever wanted her to be the person that is right for her.

Dr. Susan Love is president of the Dr. Susan Love Research Foundation, overseeing research on the cause and prevention of breast cancer. She is a former professor of surgery at Harvard Medical School and the David Geffen School of Medicine at UCLA. Known as a "founding mother" of the breast cancer advocacy movement, Love is the author of several books, including *Dr. Susan Love's Breast Book* and *Dr. Susan Love's Hormone Book: Making Informed Choices about Menopause.*

Get a Life

NANCY PELOSI

US House Democratic Leader (D-California)

Alexandra, the youngest of my five children, was the one who taught me the most when she was growing up. She was the free spirit of our family. In political terms, she was the one who was sometimes off-message.

Alexandra was the child who would sneak out of the house at midnight when she was fifteen to work the graveyard shift at the local college radio station. She was always interested in media. It was no surprise to her father and me that she became a documentary filmmaker.

One of the biggest challenges of parenting is striking the balance between wanting your child to think they can do anything and not setting them up for a fall. It's out of kindness to tell them "You're probably not going to be a concert pianist," or "You're probably not going to get the Heisman Trophy."

All of my children were fortunate to find their callings early in life.

I had a different path. I enjoyed a very full life as a wife and mother and as a very active volunteer in the Democratic Party in California before I surprised everyone by running for elected office. I have often said that I went from the kitchen to Congress. Before I led the House of Representatives, I had good training by running a house full of energetic kids.

Alexandra helped me make the decision to run in her own unique way. She was about to go into her senior year of high school in 1986 when the chance came along for me to run in a special election for a seat in my home district that was about to be vacated. I was stunned when Democratic Party officials asked me to run. At first I kept telling them, "I am not a public person; I advance other people." Even when I'd served as chair of the California Democratic Party, it had been on a volunteer basis. But people kept telling me I had to do it.

The more I thought about running the more I realized that it was something I wanted to do. My father, Thomas D'Alesandro Jr., had served nearly four decades in public office, including in Congress and as mayor of Baltimore. I knew what it meant to be a public servant. And I knew how to win elections.

But I didn't know how the last of my kids living at home would feel about me taking such a step during a momentous time in her life. I wished the election had been a year later when she'd already be off to college. But it wasn't. So I went to Alexandra and very sincerely asked her if she would be okay with me running. I told her that if she wanted me to stay home, I would.

It did not take her a nanosecond to respond.

"Mother," she said, "get a life!"

That was my daughter's way of saying that she wanted me to do what I thought was best for me. It was a kick in the pants for me to get moving on a decision that changed the rest of my life.

I think about the women of my mother's generation. She was a wonderful role model for me. She got married at nineteen and had seven children. She went to law school, but she had to drop out because four of her children got sick. Women of that generation just didn't have the opportunities that we do today—God knows what they could have accomplished. I thought about that when I became Speaker of the House.

Today, women have endless opportunities, but there is still a missing link in our evolution in society and in the economy. The evolution of women is not complete until we complete that missing link, which is child care and reproductive rights.

Many young women haven't the faintest idea how at risk issues like a women's right to choose are, which is a central issue to women's future. Some of us still have to watch over that. We are at a place where we have to be optimistic and confident but we have to be vigilant and operational to get more done.

Why should it be a question that women don't make as much as men? How could it be? It's not your boss's business what kind of contraception you use. Why are we even having a conversation about what a health plan should and should not cover?

It will be great when we get to a place where we talk about women and motherhood in the same way that we talk about men and fatherhood. Nobody ever talks about a "working dad." Being a working mom does not define you as any less of a mom.

Change is coming. It is inevitable that women will take their rightful place, because it's right for us, it's right for our families, and it's right for the country. We cannot succeed as a country unless we recognize this and make sure that every family has access to quality, affordable child care.

As I learned with Alexandra, our children are our great teachers. Our grandchildren are messengers to the future we'll never see. Leaders from all walks of life need to ensure that those children "get a life" that builds on the foundation of equality and opportunity that we foster today.

Nancy Pelosi served as Speaker of the US House of Representatives from 2007 to 2011, becoming the first woman to hold the position. She has served as House Democratic leader since 2011 and represented California's Twelfth Congressional District encompassing San Francisco since 1987. She was inducted into the National Women's Hall of Fame in 2013.

Roots and Wings

ALEXANDRA PELOSI

Filmmaker

My first child was born a few days after my mother was elected Speaker of the House of Representatives. It was a busy time for her, to say the least. But she was still calling me around the clock because the baby was due.

After the election she got on a plane and managed to get to New York just in time to be there for the birth of my son. With everything else going on at that time—at a landmark moment for women in American politics—she walks into the delivery room with an agenda, and a whole new level of security team around her now that she was Speaker.

"Let's talk about names, because you know your father has never had a grandchild named after him," my mother told me. "It would be really nice for your father if you could name him Paul."

Needless to say, my oldest son is named Paul. That's Nancy Pelosi in a nutshell. She has an incredible way of encouraging you to make the choice she wants you to make—and making you feel good about making that choice.

My mother tried to teach me many things when I was growing up—and I ignored most of it until I had children of my own. Part of growing up for me is that I now see the wisdom of my mother's ways. My mother wasn't one of those "You're the best, you're the greatest" moms. She was more honest with us about who we were and our potential.

She wasn't a tiger mom. She didn't pound us on three hours of violin a night. As long as we did our homework and were the best person we could be, that was enough.

My mother surprised us all when she decided to run for office at a time when I was the last of the five kids to be living at home. I thought that her sole purpose of being put on this earth was to drive in the car pool and make my Halloween costume. She never once said she had ambition to run for Congress, although she was always politically active as a volunteer.

I was proud of her for going for it in politics and I also admired her for another reason. After years of making three meals a day, with linens on the table and everything, she finally decided she was sick of pots and pans. She stopped cooking. It wasn't an entirely easy transition for her—for a long time she would pick up takeout from nice restaurants and put it in serving bowls so it wouldn't look like takeout. But she knew when she'd had enough.

My grandmother was a big role model in this regard. She always encouraged my sisters and me to pursue our dreams and not get married too young. It's family legend in our house that when someone would get married in Little Italy, when the bride was paraded through the streets afterward my grandmother would open up the windows and scream "sucker." She always denied it but I could imagine her doing it—and I can see her influence on my mother.

In our house, my mother always told my sisters and my brother and me that her job was to give us "roots and wings." She gave us our wings, and she still manages to call each of us every day.

My mother's achievements in public life have advanced the cause of women's equality in so many ways. She's a champion for worthy causes and she's tough enough to be one of the most powerful people in the rough-and-tumble world of national politics.

When I think about the lessons I learned from my mother, I think about my sons. Her grandson went to her swearing-in when she became Speaker. In his mind he'll never know a world in which women can't do anything. In his mind the biggest rock star he knows is his own grandmother.

―――――――――

Alexandra Pelosi is an Emmy-nominated producer and director of such HBO documentaries as *Journeys with George* (2002), *Diary of a Political Tourist* (2004), *The Trials of Ted Haggard* (2009), *Right America: Feeling Wronged—Some Voices from the Campaign Trail* (2009), *Homeless: The Motel Kids of Orange County* (2010), *Citizen USA: A 50 State Road Trip* (2011), and *Fall to Grace* (2013). Before moving into documentaries she spent ten years as a producer with *NBC News*.

Nineteen

MARIE OSMOND
Actress—singer—children's advocate

Nineteen. That's the age I was when I made a commitment to the young man I thought would become my husband. Gratefully, I was still nineteen when my mother told me something that I never expected her to say. After the shock wore off, I realized she gave me the best gift a mother can give to a daughter: the right and the courage to change my mind, to vote for my own personal happiness, no matter what.

Nineteen is also a number that redefined the future of women in America. It was the nineteenth of May of the year 1919 that there was a joint resolution of the Congress proposing the Nineteenth Amendment to the US Constitution, granting women the right to vote. With this amendment, health care, education, and working conditions for women and children were vastly improved. Our country was strengthened.

When I was nineteen, I had already been earning a paycheck for sixteen years. I had my debut performance on *The Andy Williams Show* at age three and a half and had been introduced to millions of viewers as "the youngest Osmond brother." My five older performing brothers had already preceded me onstage and on-screen as the Osmond Brothers. At age twelve, when my debut single "Paper Roses" charted at number one, my brothers were advised to drop the "Brothers" from their name to include me on international tours. By age fourteen, I had been paired with my brother Donny, and had the number-one variety show on television, airing every Friday night. By age nineteen, it was difficult for me to go anywhere without the press in pursuit. Most young women, at that age, want to get out, express themselves, and experience the world. I craved the opposite: to have a home of my own and a husband, and to start a family.

I believed that I was ready at nineteen. He was bright, charming in public, very handsome, and he could even sing really well. I had known him for more than three years, first as a friend and then, eventually, dating. One day he proposed. I accepted. I started making the wedding plans. I began drawing up the look for my dream wedding dress and called my designer to have it made. I found the perfect shoes, invitations, put a down payment on a place to hold the reception, and even preordered and paid for a gorgeous cake.

A week before our wedding invitations were to be sent, it became increasingly clear to me that my "happily ever after" dream was turning into a "wait just a minute" reality.

I woke to the fact that my fiancé's idea of "wedded bliss" was for me to back-burner my performing career and use my influence and efforts to forward his acting and singing career. It appeared that home and family would be something for the distant future.

Suddenly, I felt scared and full of regret about the idea of getting married. I knew what I had to do, ultimately, but I dreaded it on many levels.

First, I had to deal with the emotion and pain of telling him that it was over. Then I was concerned about the backlash from the press since a big announcement had already been released. But, mostly, I worried about how my parents would react, considering that I was the one who proclaimed that this young man was right for me. They had both had their doubts, but didn't want to deny me my feelings. They had gone along with my wedding planning, contributing to each expense along the way.

Soon after my eye-opening realization, I sat at the kitchen table with my mother while she was sorting out her canning jars for the boxes of fresh peaches stacked nearby. My parents had a lifelong appreciation for frugality. They always chose to garden and can their own fruit and vegetables. Knowing that my parents rarely wasted a single resource made what I had to say even harder.

My voice was hesitant as I told my mother: "I made a mistake. I can't marry him. I know we can't return the things we've ordered for the wedding and that means we will lose thousands of dollars. I'm very sorry."

I waited for my mother to respond with disappointment or firmness about how I should have made sure he was "the one" before I made wedding plans. I thought she might express frustration about money that could never be recovered for items that could never be used. She did the opposite. After listening, she broke into a wide smile, jumped to her feet, and wrapped her arms around me. "That's the best money we've ever spent! . . . Especially if it bought you the wisdom to follow your true heart," she said. "I'm so pleased that you had the insight to not go through with a marriage that wasn't right for you. I don't care what it cost. It didn't cost you your long-term happiness."

It was a lesson that stayed with me, reinforced by the way my parents role-modeled a healthy marriage: partners with equal, but different, strengths who supported each other fully. But this was a lesson I never shared with anyone because it seemed so personal to my life.

My daughter Rachael was nineteen when she moved with me and the younger kids to Las Vegas, where she works designing costumes for "Donny & Marie" at the Flamingo Hotel. Over the next two years she casually dated several young men she met through church and work, but nothing ever became serious.

When the show went on tour to Chicago for a month, she met an entrepreneurial young man, named Gabriel, from a huge family, with a great sense of humor and a lot of personal motivation. They hit it off, instantly. They tried to date, long distance, for about six months, but finally it became too much of a constant struggle, with 2,000 miles between them.

Rachael went on to date another young man, who was in college and seemed to share her goals for the future. After dating for about five months, he proposed and she accepted.

The wedding planning began in full, and we had many mother-daughter shopping trips so she could try on dresses and pick out invitations, bridesmaid outfits, and more.

As life, or perhaps genetics, would have it, history repeated itself for my sweet daughter.

A week before the invitations were to be sent she came to me, perching on the edge of my bed one late night to talk. She felt, in her heart, that he wasn't the man who should be her husband. She began to weep quietly about having to break up with him and also the money I had already spent on her wedding and her dress.

I hugged her as my mother's words became my own: "It's the best money I've ever spent," I assured her. "I wouldn't care if you came to me the morning of your wedding and told me that it was a mistake. I'm so happy that you had the insight to know it was a mistake before you made the actual commitment. This experience has given you a great amount of priceless wisdom."

Once her Chicago beau, Gabriel, heard the wedding was off, he came to visit. He told her that he had never stopped loving her and she admitted that she felt the same way. To prove his dedication to my daughter, he relocated to Las Vegas, found an apartment and a job, studied her faith thoroughly, and ended up becoming a member of our church. On Christmas Day, 2012, they got married. As a couple, they remind me so much of my mother and dad.

The wisdom my mother gave to me that I want to pass on to my four daughters is to know that they always have the right to change their minds, especially when it comes to their personal happiness, whether it involves friendships, potential partners, and even career choices. I don't want my daughters to feel they must strive to break the glass ceiling in business, when perhaps their true hearts call to them to stay home to nurture children.

In the same realm, they shouldn't leave a career that they love, unless it's their own decision.

Just as women in 1919 strengthened our country by winning the right to vote, young women today can strengthen the nucleus of each family with their personal vote to be true to themselves, first.

From our daughters' happiness comes the next generation of girls who will walk in truth, love selflessly because they know who they are, and stand in a strong, yet feminine, confidence that truly will rock the world.

———

Marie Osmond began performing on the national stage at the age of three when she made her TV debut on *The Andy Williams Show*. She logged a hit single, "Paper Roses," at the age of twelve and has since recorded more than thirty-five albums. In addition to her work on TV, stage, and film, Osmond is cofounder of the Children's Miracle Network and the founder of Marie Osmond Dolls. She has authored two bestselling books, *Behind the Smile* and *Might As Well Laugh About It Now*.

The Wall

DR. JULIET GARCÍA
University president

When I was named the first Latina female president of a college or university in the United States in 1986, I sought out the wisdom of several experienced elders to help me frame what the most important part of my work was to become. One wise mentor and fellow college president explained that he thought the most important part of his job was to sustain our country's democracy: to take in the next wave of immigrants and help them become educated and vested in our democratic system. He believed that if he did this well, our newest citizens would nurture, defend, and sustain our democracy. The moment I heard his words, I knew that his vision would become my own.

It was with great astonishment, then, that two decades later, after many years of successfully serving as president and having graduated thousands of first-generation college graduates, I found myself being sued by the United States government—the same government I believed I was sustaining. This was a trying time for me, and I leaned on the support of my family and friends. In the middle of the post-9/11 drama playing out on my university campus, no one rallied to my side with as much determination as my daughter, Paulita García Rico.

The University of Texas at Brownsville sits just one block from the Rio Grande River, the politically imposed border between the United States and Mexico that empties into the Gulf of Mexico just thirty miles south of the university campus at South Padre Island. Living on the border had always been an advantage for those of us living and working in the binational and cross-border region, with a vibrant and dynamic flow of goods and services, relatives living on both sides of the river, and the tapestry woven by the interface of two languages and cultures. It is a place that historically more closely resembled a Mediterranean port city than a typical city in Texas.

But that was before 9/11. Afterward, life as we had known it changed dramatically. Passengers boarding planes in Brownsville had to go through the new security measures and were subjected to questioning by officers from the Department of Homeland Security. In addition, we were now asked for proof of citizenship. What had once been a routine trip across the border from Brownsville to Matamoros to shop was now discouraged by the new constraints of additional security procedures that often slowed traffic to almost a halt.

One of the most intrusive outcomes of the new security initiatives was a newly enacted law, the Secure Fence Act that required the US government to build an 18-foot-high wall across pockets of the Texas-Mexico border.

In the fall of 2007, our university was asked to allow the Department of Homeland Security to build a portion of this fence on our campus, essentially placing more than 120 acres of our property on the south side of the border wall. I refused to sign their request for permission to proceed. As a result, we were sued by the Department of Homeland Security, spent two years in a legal dispute, and appeared in federal court three times.

The case quickly caught the attention of national and international news media, bringing unwelcome fame to the university and all of us involved in the dispute. All of a sudden we found ourselves in conflict with the very government that we had all thought shared our core values.

My daughter, who is now a mother herself to two daughters, was faced with her own decision to make: whether to support her mother during this controversial period or to quietly steal away and hide until the issue was settled. She never hesitated for a moment. She took up the cause personally, had bumper stickers made opposing the border wall and made sure people displayed them prominently on their cars or at their businesses. My teenage granddaughters quickly joined her and distributed bumper stickers to their friends at school.

I'm sure no one wants to see their mother or their grandmother sued in federal court by the US government. While I was blessed with receiving support from many, none meant more to me than the gift of unconditional support from my own daughter and granddaughters. I had had many occasions to be proud of them before, but during this most difficult time, my pride for them grew immensely.

On July 31, 2008, after a grueling period of being under the harsh spotlight of public controversy and tough negotiations with federal officials, US District Court Judge Andrew Hanen ruled that the federal government not be allowed to build the 18-foot-high fence on university property. Instead, he allowed us to design a 10-foot-high fence that, instead of looking ominous, looked more like it belonged at a country club.

To celebrate the occasion, hundreds of people helped us plant flowering vines on the fence to signal the importance of maintaining a peaceful coexistence with our friends in Mexico.

I recently had occasion to sit on a panel with Drew Faust, the president of Harvard. She talked about the bombing incident during the 2013 Boston Marathon. She said that most people, when they heard the explosions, began to run away, as fast as they could. But not everybody ran away. Some people chose to run toward the explosions and returned to see how they could help the injured.

When my daughter made the decision to support me in the very public and uncomfortable confrontation with the Department of Homeland Security, she also chose to run toward—not away from—the controversy and the important issues it represented.

There is always much to learn from these moments, but chief among them is that the toughest battles in our lives are those we learn from the most. They are the ones that make us surface our courage. My daughter and my granddaughters chose to run toward—not away from—the battle. They chose to surface their own courage.

———————

Dr. Juliet García is a pioneering academician who has dedicated her career to expanding access to education through innovation, experimentation, and efficiency. She became the first Latina to lead a college or university in the United States when she was named president of Texas Southmost College in 1986. In 1992, she spearheaded the drive to create a new university, the University of Texas at Brownsville, and served as its president for twenty-three years. Since 2014, Dr. García has served as executive director of the University of Texas Institute of the Americas.

Faith, Family, and Country

JEHAN SADAT, PhD

Humanitarian-activist

When I was growing up, women in both the East and West were confined by traditional practices that dictated a woman's place was in the home, regardless of personal ambition and education. My mother, a teacher in her native England, did not work outside of our home in Cairo. Neither did my Egyptian aunties whose upbringing was vastly different from that of my mother. Yet together they instilled within me a sense of independence, a passion for justice, and a deep devotion to my faith, family, and country—the same values I tried to instill in my children.

My greatest accomplishment is my children: one boy, Gamal, and three girls, Loubna, Noha, and Jehan. We have lived through some difficult times, through wars and revolution and the assassination of their father. Each of them was born when Egypt was at war with Israel, a period spanning more than thirty years. Just as they learned the meaning of the Call to Prayer as it echoed through the streets of Cairo, they learned the wail of an air raid siren meant for them to go quickly to the nearest shelter.

Growing up in such an atmosphere was extremely stressful. Adding additional pressure was the fact that their father, Anwar Sadat, was the president of our nation. They were fearful but not panicked when they heard tanks rumbling toward our home, not knowing whether they were friend or foe. They could see the people protesting in the streets from their bedroom balconies. They were familiar with the sound of random gunfire. They lived every day with the possibility of their father being killed or their mother being kidnapped. While their lives were less than normal in so many ways, our home was full of love for God, country, and one another.

I was a young mother, having married a jobless revolutionary hero when I was sixteen. I postponed my education for the sake of my family. It was, therefore, important to me that each of my children, especially my daughters, earned a university degree. When they began university, I did, too, at the same university. I was forty, a mother, and the wife of the president, with many duties and obligations but also a determination to set the right example for my children as well as the women of Egypt. I awoke before dawn and studied hours after everyone had gone to bed. When I sat for my oral examinations, my husband and my children were in the audience. Afterward, my youngest daughter, Jehan, told one of the professors they had treated me too harshly. She understood when he explained they had been harsh so no one could say I had been evaluated differently, that

I had been given my degree because of my husband. This was important to me too. It was in keeping with the principles and values I had taught my children when they were young.

My children were raised with the understanding that in the eyes of God, men and women are equal and should be treated with mutual respect. One does not have dominion over the other. My daughters have never considered themselves as less than a man, just different, and my son has never believed himself superior. I taught them little things such as not crossing their legs in front of adults or even sighing when asked to do something, how to say, "Yes, sir" and "No, sir" and "Yes, ma'am" and "No, ma'am" to all adults. I taught them to think and freely express themselves but always with respect. I was strict but not unreasonable; I had high expectations of my children.

Once when my son kept putting off getting his hair cut, I cut it myself and not in a good way. He was devastated. Equally upset with how I had treated her brother, Jehan decided she and Gamal would cut the fur of our pet monkey in the same style. Actually it was much worse, but because I knew Jehan was showing sympathy toward her brother, I did not punish either of them.

I wanted my children to feel how much their parents believed in God, how much we loved and respected each other, and how much we loved our country. I wanted them to be proud of me, to see that I was doing as I was telling them to do. When I went to offer condolences to bereaved friends, I took them. When I went to hospitals to comfort our wounded soldiers, I took them. When I went to help the poor women of the villages earn their own money to contribute to the welfare of their families, I took them. I wanted them with me to see and feel the pain and suffering of the poor, illiterate people of our country. I wanted them to learn how to make a difference in the lives of others. I wanted them to know that only in giving to others do we ourselves receive.

My children and I have shared great joy. We have also suffered together. We have lived under a kind of house arrest when curfews and roadblocks prevented us from being together. We have smelled the black smoke of burning tires and the acrid smell of tear gas floating past our windows. We have endured terrorists invading our country, killing our people in our streets and squares. Our eyes cry and our hearts ache as our beloved Egypt struggles and strives to restore the rule of law and establish a democracy that represents and protects the rights of all of the people.

On June 30, 2013, when 40 million Egyptians took to the streets in support of our military and interim government, I stood on a balcony in my home overlooking a major thoroughfare leading to Tahrir Square. With one hand, I was waving the Egyptian flag, and with the other, I was waving to the marchers. My heart was full of patriotism and pride, the former for the millions who marched to save us from chaos and the latter for my daughters who marched with them. My daughters have not been confined by traditions. They have a sense of independence, a passion for justice, and a deep devotion to their faith, families, and country. They have learned their lessons well. My children know that faith, family, and country will sustain them. Love of God, family, and country are as steadfast as the pyramids and as constant as the Nile.

————

Dr. Jehan Sadat, a pioneering advocate for children and women's rights in the Muslim world, is an internationally renowned proponent of peace and human rights. Currently, she is a senior fellow with the Anwar Sadat Chair for Peace and Development at the University of Maryland, College Park. Dr. Sadat is the widow of Egyptian president Anwar Sadat, who served from 1970 to his assassination on October 6, 1981.

Role Reversals

MADELEINE ALBRIGHT

Diplomat

I am forever grateful to have had the opportunity to represent the United States of America. In the course of that service, I was known as an ambassador, as a secretary, and, ultimately, as a breaker of glass ceilings.

At the peak of my diplomatic career, I may have been the leader of the US State Department, but I still had to answer to my three daughters when it came to my spending habits. And they scrutinized every penny.

"Mom, did you really need another pair of shoes?" my daughter Anne would ask while reviewing my bills for the month. My daughters took over the management of my finances after I became ambassador to the United Nations in 1993 and secretary of state in 1997. With all the travel those jobs require, I had no time to manage my own affairs. That amounted to a role reversal that was illuminating for all of us.

One of the tensest moments during my tenure as UN ambassador came in 1996 during a trip to Croatia, less than four months after the signing of the historic Dayton Peace Agreement that brought an end to the war in Bosnia and Herzegovina. I led a UN delegation to see firsthand what life was like in the Balkans under the accord.

At one stop, I got out of my car to walk through the Serb-held city of Vukovar. As we approached an open-air market I heard people yelling insults. "You whore" sounds just as awful in Serbo-Croatian as it does in English. As we returned to our cars, stones began to fly and our motorcade was pretty banged up as we left the area.

Later that day CNN ran a report with the headline "Albright Stoned in Serbia." That prompted my daughters to make frantic calls to the State Department to see if I was okay.

When I got home a few days later, I got an earful from my girls.

"Mom, this is outrageous. You can't go off to dangerous places and not tell us what you are doing. You're being very irresponsible." It sounded like something I might have said to them as teenagers if they had broken curfew. They were very upset with me for making them worry.

These experiences reinforced the strength of our bond as a family—something I tried to demonstrate to my daughters not with words so much as by my actions. The hardest thing that working women face is the struggle of balancing the needs of your job and the needs of your family. But when push comes to shove, family always comes first. The care and concern my daughters have shown for me in their adulthood tells me that message was received loud and clear.

My twins, Alice and Anne, were teenagers and Katie was a preteen when I began to work outside the home. I was nearly forty when I completed my PhD in public law and government from Columbia University. By then I was a single mother.

My timing was fortunate, because just as women were starting to make strides in the Title IX era, my credentials were in order. When Senator Edmund Muskie hired me to be his chief legislative analyst, I wasn't presented on Capitol Hill as "Muskie's friend Madeleine" but as "Dr. Albright."

As my career advanced, the balancing act inevitably became harder. I was often away from home. It was an adjustment for all of us. But the worst pressure I felt came not from my daughters but from other women. So many women made me feel awful about my choices. I always say every woman's middle name is "guilt" because we are so judgmental of one another.

For years, there was an unspoken rule in Washington that there was only one slot, maybe two, for a woman on any team. That feeling created an unhealthy competitive dynamic among women with big ambitions and a disincentive to help one another.

Today, thankfully, there are many more people who have come to realize we're all better off if there's more than one woman in the room. I believe those of us at the top have an obligation to mentor and support one another. Hillary Clinton did that for me. I wouldn't have become secretary of state without Hillary pushing President Bill Clinton to give me the job—not because I was a woman but because she was confident I was the best person to articulate his foreign policy views.

It seems unbelievable in hindsight, but back then there were people who genuinely questioned whether a woman could handle the job of secretary of state. There was concern that the Arab states would not accept a female in the role. Some foreign press reports on my appointment were brutal. The Serbs, for instance, identified me as "elderly, but dangerous."

But attitudes change. This was driven home to me by an observation made a few years ago by my youngest granddaughter.

"What's the big deal with Grandma Maddy being secretary of state?" she asked. "Only girls are secretary of state." I realized then that in her lifetime that was largely true. After my tenure ended in 2001, Condoleezza Rice served from 2005 to 2009 and Hillary Clinton from 2009 to 2013.

Now that my daughters have families and careers of their own, we've talked a lot about how it was for them growing up when my career took me away from home. They are amazed at how much time we managed to spend together despite my schedule. I'm proud that the professional paths taken by Alice, Anne, and Katherine have involved aspects of public service and giving back for the greater good.

The question "How did you do it all?" may be the biggest compliment a mother can get from her adult children. It's freed me from those nagging feelings of guilt, once and for all.

———

Madeleine Albright is a professor of diplomacy at the Georgetown University School of Foreign Service. From 1997 to 2001, Albright was the first woman to serve as secretary of state. From 1993 to 1997, she served as the US ambassador to the United Nations. Earlier, Albright was a member of President Jimmy

Carter's National Security Council and White House staff, and she served as chief legislative assistant to US Senator Edmund Muskie. She is the author of five books, including the 2003 autobiography *Madam Secretary: A Memoir*. In 2012, Albright was awarded the Presidential Medal of Freedom.

Listening in the Rowboat

JOANNA KERNS
Actress-director

My father was always proud to say that he had four sons, but two of them happened to be girls. He was the one who gave my sister and me the confidence that we were capable of doing anything a man could do. This influence made me a feminist before I knew there was such a word.

The professions that my sister, Donna de Varona, and I have chosen proved that we learned well from our father. Donna was an Olympian and a gold medalist in swimming in the 1964 Olympics. She went on to become a pioneering female sportscaster for network television.

I went into acting and later directing for prime-time television—a field that remains dominated by men. I had the good fortune in my career to land a leading role on a successful sitcom, ABC's *Growing Pains*, which led me to many other opportunities. But my work as a TV mom at times caused real-life pain for my daughter, Ashley. The hard work of getting through this only-in-Hollywood challenge has tested and ultimately strengthened the bond between us.

I spent the last half of the 1980s and the early 1990s playing one of America's favorite moms, giving advice and encouragement to my TV children and the millions of children who watched us, always with humor and just enough wisdom to make sense. But in my personal life things weren't so perfect. I was a single mom, newly separated, and in the process of divorce. Ashley was seven and weathering first grade with a mom who was suddenly a famous mom. Kids in school, thinking she had it better than they did, could be mean. She suffered isolation because of the divorce. She not only lost the presence of her father from our household but in her mind she lost part of me as well.

Ashley's way of handling all of these overwhelming emotions was to pretend she was a cat. Sometimes it was easier for her to hiss or purr at me. Sometimes words simply weren't enough. I didn't always know what Ashley was feeling but I certainly understood the cat. So did the girl who was bullying her at lunch one day and cut in front of Ashley in line for milk. Ashley hissed, the claws came out, and the next thing I knew my daughter and I were sitting in the principal's office. She had been suspended.

On the way home in the car we had one of those rowboat conversations where you don't look at each other. Tearfully, she told me how sad she was that her dad was gone, how lonely she felt knowing things were going to change, and how angry she was at me because I had a whole other family at work. Worse, all the kids at school thought I was supernice and funny all the time.

"And you are not funny!" Ashley defiantly declared.

I gave it a few beats and then asked quite seriously: "Never?"

We both started to laugh. Even at age seven, Ashley knew how to get to me.

In that moment, I was nothing like my TV character. I didn't have any funny advice to dispense. But I learned from Ashley that sometimes the best advice is no advice. Sometimes it's best to just be that other person in the rowboat, ready and willing to listen.

I did tell her, however, that the cat could hiss but not scratch.

Like me, Ashley has grown up to be a proud feminist. She went to New York University, graduated magna cum laude, and went on to Loyola Law School. She passed the bar on the first round, practiced law, became an avid swing dancer, and fell in love with scuba diving before becoming seriously ill in 2008.

From the time Ashley got sick, she and I have traveled the country and scoured the Internet searching for an accurate diagnosis for the onset of the crushing fatigue, joint pain, and flulike symptoms she has suffered, causing her to give up her hard-earned career. Our health care system is brutal when you are sick. The system is its own kind of bully—excluding, ignoring, and pushing the sick to the back of the line. I am her advocate and sometimes I want to hiss, scratch, and push back. But I know that does not work.

I tell Ashley that she is not her illness. She is a strong, beautiful woman with amazing intelligence, and we will not stop until we find the answer to her mystery. Drawing on the Buddhist practice of non-contention, I tell her to "be a curtain":

se moments when a doctor, health care worker, or
ling but ignorant friend says something uninten-
urtful land like a tennis ball into a curtain. Let that
tennis ball drop to a dead stop on the floor instead of slamming
against a hard wall and bouncing back. Don't hiss and scratch;
be the curtain.

Our children are forever our children, even when they're
grown. But it's still difficult to know what our job as a parent is
as the child gets older. I still want to fix things that sometimes
can't be fixed. I still have the instinct to reassure her that everything is going to be okay, no matter what.

But what I actually do most of all is sit in that rowboat and
try to listen. It's one of the hardest things for a mother to do,
but it's the best advice I can ever give.

––––––––

Joanna Kerns is an accomplished actress and director. She
costarred from 1985 to 1992 in the hit ABC domestic comedy
Growing Pains. She has also been seen in such movies as *Knocked
Up* and *Girl, Interrupted*. As a director, her long list of credits
includes *Ally McBeal*, *ER*, *Pretty Little Liars*, *Scrubs*, *Grey's Anatomy*,
and *The Fosters*.

The Dalai Lama's Slam Dunk

GLORIA ESTEFAN

Entertainer-entrepreneur

It was a lovely October day, the kind that gives me what I call "autumn feeling," when the light in the afternoon starts to change and the air feels slightly crisper. To add to my joy, I had received an email telling me that the Dalai Lama was coming to my alma mater, the University of Miami, to speak on the subject of happiness.

There was no way I was going to miss this and I really wanted my sixteen-year-old daughter, Emily, to hear what he had to say. She was then a junior in high school, a year when everything increases in importance and has a real impact on your future. Grades would count more than ever and she'd be forced to make big decisions such as what colleges to apply to and what extracurricular activities would merit her time—in addition to doing her schoolwork and studying for the SATs or ACTs.

I could clearly see that Em was under a lot of pressure since she was both in her school's Contemporary Music Ensemble and Jazz Band and played point guard on her high school varsity basketball team. At the time she was just about to begin the team's grueling, three-hour daily practice schedule on top of several hours a week of rehearsal for her musical commitments. I knew Emily was an incredibly mature, resourceful, organized, and disciplined human being, but I could also sense there was something she hadn't verbalized. Being her usual responsible self, she worried that attending the Dalai Lama's speech would make her miss class and cause her to be late for her first basketball practice of the season. The coach was very strict about being on time and she didn't want to start off on the wrong foot.

I volunteered to explain to her school principal the importance of her attending the speech. Hearing the Dalai Lama speak is a rare opportunity in and of itself, but Emily would also be meeting the Dalai Lama, whom I had had the honor to meet and converse with four years before. He had left me impressed and awestruck and I wanted her to experience something she'd remember forever. What I didn't know was that it would change her life that very day and put her at a crossroads where she'd be forced to make one of life's first big decisions.

Backstage, in the presence of His Holiness, I could see Em taking in every utterance, watching his body language, observing him as she tends to do with people that she finds fascinating and respects. Afterward, we went to our seats for the speech and for two hours we were hanging on his every word. His message was clear, simple, and profound, and it felt like everyone in that arena was transformed in some way that day. Leaving the event we found ourselves in bumper-to-bumper traffic, making Em's fear of being late a clear and present danger. She was agitated and worried and, though I tried to calm her down by offering to talk to the coach, she didn't like me running interference in matters she felt she needed to face on her own. We dropped her at school only ten minutes late, thinking everything was fine.

At around seven p.m., as I headed back to school to pick her up, she called me, very upset, saying we needed to talk in person. My heart started pounding in the way that only a parent's can when they hear those words from their child. I sped up and immediately began going over countless scenarios in my head until I had to tell myself to take it easy and wait to hear what she had to say. I pulled up to the gym parking lot, she threw herself into the car, looked at me, took a deep breath, and started to cry. I can count on one hand the times that my stoic baby girl has cried in her life, so I was blown away. I asked if her coach had yelled or been rude because she was late, she said no, then it all poured out.

The Dalai Lama's speech had hit home. His words about happiness had made her realize she was no longer happy playing basketball. The girl who had loved and dedicated herself to basketball for six years and had single-handedly won her middle school's first tournament in eighty-four years by scoring 72 points in three games was finding herself getting angry when the time came to go to practice. It felt like she was wasting her time, better spent making music, which she could happily do for countless hours. She was concerned that her GPA would drop because there was not enough time to study and she'd maintained a 4.0 her entire school career.

Then I reminded her of something her home-room teacher had said at freshman orientation two years before—to try different things in the first two years of high school. Then, by the time they were juniors, hopefully find their passion and devote time to it rather than spread themselves too thin. I told her I was proud of her for being mature enough to realize that a choice had to be made and she had to be brave enough to make it. Between sobs she said she didn't want to let her coach or her teammates down, and she felt bad taking up a spot on the team that should go to someone who still had the passion to play. She was afraid of what Coach's reaction might be when she told him she wanted off the team.

I asked her to look at me, and with as much tranquility as I could muster, explained to her that she needed to tell her coach, in person, exactly what she had just told me. There were three possible ways he could react:

A. He would be the teacher I hoped he was and would congratulate her for putting academics first and for being honest; B. He could try to guilt her into staying for the sake of the team; or C. He could yell at her, call her a quitter, and kick her out of his office.

I laughed and told her I'd be shocked if "C" actually happened and that facing Coach and decisively taking the reins of her own life would strengthen her belief in herself and her ability to make good decisions in the future. Staring straight ahead she said, "That's going to be very hard, but I'm doing it tomorrow!" After a pause she added: "Mom, I feel like a huge weight has been lifted from my shoulders."

The next afternoon, while she spoke to Coach, I waited in the gym parking lot, motor running per her request, in case she needed to make a quick getaway. She jumped into my car all smiles, back to her usual happy self.

"He was great, Mom," she informed me. "He told me he was disappointed, but he understood. Then he shook my hand and told me I would always have a place on the team if I changed my mind. Please thank the Dalai Lama for me." She chuckled. "I'M SO HAPPY!"

I told my daughter, "Then I am too!"

———————

Gloria Estefan is a seven-time Grammy winner who has sold more than 100 million albums worldwide. As an actress and entrepreneur, Estefan has been a driving force in the crossover popularity of Latin music. Estefan and her husband, Emilio Estefan, are producers of the biographical Broadway musical *On Your Feet!*

Walking and Talking

NANNERL O. KEOHANE
Academician–political theorist

Unlike many mothers, I have become closer to my stepdaughter Sarah in her adulthood than when she was growing up.

Our best opportunities to be together and talk about important issues have come during her college years and after. Sarah is now a successful executive, a volunteer for a number of good causes, and a dedicated mother of three children.

Sarah and I love the outdoors. Many of our best talks have come while we were walking around Lake Waban in Wellesley, Massachusetts. We often discuss some challenge in my work or hers, as well as the activities and accomplishments of her kids. Sarah tells me that she particularly recalls three pieces of advice that came from these walks.

When I became president of Wellesley College in 1981, the Investment Committee of the Board of Trustees, on which

I served ex officio, met each month at the Somerset Club on Beacon Hill. This had been the appointed meeting place for many years. Several members of the board were members of the club, and its facilities were excellent. There was just one catch: women were not allowed in the club except through a basement entrance, coming through a frilly pink Ladies' Parlor and taking a special elevator upstairs to be escorted to the meeting room. Even though all the presidents of Wellesley had been women, somehow this hadn't been an issue for my predecessors. It surely was for me, however, as an ardent second-wave feminist.

At the end of the first meeting of the committee, I raised the issue of the basement entrance, politely but firmly. My colleagues agreed that this was not appropriate, and one of the board members offered to host the meetings around the corner at the Union Club, which welcomed women. When I described this compromise to Sarah, the lesson she took from that was: "You need to be in the room to make real changes." Earn your spot at the table and then press for improvements. A few years later, I was happy to tell Sarah during another walk that the Somerset Club had revised its policies and that I and other women on the board were happily able to attend events in those hallowed halls.

Another instance involved the lesson of giving careful consideration to all professional opportunities that come your way, even those that seem to offer only an upside. In the mid-1980s, I was asked to join the board of a prominent corporation, one that virtually anyone would consider a prize post. I surely thought of it in this way, but I was also concerned about the demands on my time and possible conflicts of interest with my day job. I spent several days pondering the invitation, asking advice from my board chair and family members. I eventually accepted the invitation and have always been very glad I did. But Sarah recalls learning from this experience that you don't always have to accept the first offer that comes along and the importance of taking the time to think through the possible consequences.

During those Wellesley years, one of my most important commitments as president was to take the contributions of all members of the community seriously, no matter what jobs they held. I spent time with the buildings and grounds personnel, fascinated by and grateful for their work on the facilities, the gardens, and the beautiful campus. I visited them occasionally in their workplaces, and greeted them on campus. At one point, I got a blue work shirt with my name embroidered on it, the same kind of shirt that these workers wore on the job. To Sarah, this was a vivid example of the importance of being a leader who connects with everyone in the organization, not just the people at the top of the hierarchy.

Like most women of the generation that came of age in the 1980s and 1990s, Sarah didn't consider herself a feminist when she was growing up. She thought, as most of her friends did, that feminism was something from the past. All the battles had been fought and won, and her generation would reap the benefits and move on to new heights without worrying about gender issues. But her views changed after she graduated from college and began tackling the challenges of the "real world." The conversations on our lakeside walks were part of her personal growth as a feminist, a label that she now proudly accepts as her own.

I benefit from these conversations as much as Sarah does.

She is a thoughtful and supportive interlocutor, and I learn from her practical perspective and experience in fields that are quite different from my own. We are convinced that some of the best mother-daughter communication is destined to come in adulthood, when the relationship dynamic is that of equals providing mutual support and growth.

———

Nannerl O. Keohane is a Laurance S. Rockefeller Distinguished Visiting Professor of Public Affairs at Princeton University's Center for Human Values. She previously served as president of Wellesley College and of Duke University.

Natural Talents

JENNIFER DULSKI
Technology entrepreneur—social business leader

I remember so clearly when my younger daughter, then nine years old, piped up from the backseat of the car:

"Mommy, I want to be famous."

My immediate thought was "Oh no"—or probably something much stronger than that, if I'm being honest. Visions of the rise and crushing fall of reality TV stardom ran through my mind.

Trying not to jump to conclusions, I asked her what she wanted to be famous for. When she said she didn't know, I offered: "You could win the Nobel Prize—that would make you famous."

It was not my finest moment. And then there was silence.

So I decided to take a step back and take the conversation more seriously. "What are you good at doing?" I asked.

"Well, I'm good at resolving conflicts between my friends, and I'm good at making people feel happy when they're sad."

It was an incredible moment. At nine years old, she so clearly understood her natural talents, and was so articulate about them. And she was also clearly right; as I thought about it, every teacher we'd ever spoken to and every report card she'd received testified to exactly those talents.

Now that she's a teenager, my daughter has become the *de facto* mediator in our household. Whenever there's an argument at home, she will leave the room and come back with a document detailing how each of us is involved, and the role we can each play in improving the situation. She's the one her friends go to for advice. She can invariably cheer people up, even in the toughest of circumstances. No one told her how to do it. She just sees the world in a different light, and views problems from a different perspective. That is a talent.

So the question is: What can she do with it? We talk about this regularly, and she knows that having identified her true talents, the opportunities are massive. She could become a therapist, a human resources executive, a global conflict mediator, or any number of other things. Whatever path she chooses, understanding her natural talents so early presents an incredible chance to spend her life doing something she is really good at—setting her up for success and leadership.

My older daughter is a strong student and excels in many subjects, but what makes her good at those things are her underlying natural talents—patience, focus, and careful observation. When she was just three years old, she would come home from preschool every day with several "punching jobs," where she punched out the outline of a design using a tiny needle. The patience and focus required to do that for several hours a day at such a young age was a talent—the kind of talent that might make her a good scientist, photographer, or other careers that require patience and focus. While her talents are different from her sister's, she also has a plethora of options available to her that would be a good fit for a future career.

It's an incredible feeling to see my children demonstrate this much self-awareness at a young age. I was in my early thirties before I really understood what I was good at. My path to the right career involved a demotion and a few attempts at running a start-up before finding something that was the right way to leverage my own talent.

Since I became aware of the concept of natural talents, I love spotting them in the members of my team, and talking to people about how their talents always have a potentially important application. Imagine how we could change the world if we all recognized our innate strengths and used them for good.

While I never found out what my daughter wanted to be famous for, I love knowing that she has a deep understanding of her talents and her capacity to be really good at something. And who knows, her talent for resolving conflict may just win her the Nobel Peace Prize after all.

Jennifer Dulski is the president and COO of Change.org, the world's largest social change platform, with more than 100 million users in 196 countries. She spent nine years at Yahoo! before becoming cofounder and CEO of The Dealmap, which was acquired by Google in 2011—making Dulski the first female entrepreneur to sell a company to Google. She spent nearly two years at Google before joining Change.org in January 2013. Dulski writes about leadership, management, and entrepreneurship for LinkedIn Influencers, *Fortune,* and the *Huffington Post*, among other media outlets.

Freedom of Choice

DR. MARCIA McNUTT

Geophysicist-editor

Wham! It was like Ashley had hit a wall. She had cruised through summer, enjoying some free time, hanging out with friends, making a little money at her summer job, and venturing forth on a few dates with good-looking boys. It was late August, and she just couldn't face the prospect of returning to the girls' school she had attended for the past six years. Using a mixture of logic and emotion, she implored me to allow her to attend the local public school instead. She calmly recited the list of students who had done well there, going on to good colleges. She used tears to punctuate her anticipated emotional trauma if forced to spend one more year in a highly competitive, single-sex environment.

I was torn. I was the product of a highly competitive, all-girls school myself. Over the years, I had been astonished at how many high-achieving women I had met in my own age cohort had also been fortunate enough to experience that environment, where everything was possible for women because no one ever told you otherwise and where women were always in leadership positions. I had also been saddened to hear of how many of those institutions were no longer exclusively for women. I felt lucky to have found such a place for Ashley in Santa Catalina School in Monterey, California. And of course I had already paid her tuition for the year.

On the other hand, the reason I had sent her to such a school was to raise a strong, independent young woman, one confident to make her own informed choices. Ashley was seventeen and would be going to college in a year. After six years at Santa Catalina, if she was not capable of making a good choice by now, surely she would not be a year from now. Other Catalina parents were appalled when they learned that just one week into the school year, I had told Ashley that if she wished, she could withdraw from school, and I would enroll her in the local public school. But Ashley was elated. After years of uniforms, she asked her sister Dana to help her pick out a first-day-of-school outfit. Ashley had dreams of football games, a widening circle of friends, and much less homework.

By noon of Ashley's first day at her new school I got a call from her saying that she had already contacted the headmistress at Catalina to let her know that she would be returning the following day. She stopped by Catalina to pick up books and homework assignments she had missed on account of her public school detour. Needless to say, our local public school had not lived up to her expectations. Ashley had found the students unprepared and inattentive, and the teachers burned out. It didn't help that her late enrollment meant that she was assigned to classes that had space rather than classes that were most appropriate for her. She returned to Catalina with a renewed commitment and appreciation for her opportunity.

The following spring, on a perfect day in June, I had the honor to be the commencement speaker at Ashley's graduation from Santa Catalina. I listed for the graduating seniors and their proud families all of the achievements that had been exclusively male on that day, thirtysomething years ago, when I graduated from high school, but now were women's achievements as well. I went on to describe some of the high peaks left to scale, perfect targets for young women with independence, leadership, and good judgment.

Ashley went off to Stanford that fall, and she has excelled at everything she puts her mind to ever since.

But as much as same-sex education worked for Ashley, it's not a one-size-fits-all proposition for all girls. My family is living proof of this. Ashley's identical twin sister, Dana, attended Santa Catalina for junior high but chose a coed school for senior high. Ashley and Dana's older sister, Meredith, attended coed institutions throughout her academic life.

Dana and Meredith are equally amazing as Ashley in terms of drive, independence, and self-confidence. While I remain a firm believer in the value of women's educational institutions, I believe it's even more important for parents to give their daughters the freedom to blossom into strong, independent individuals. Part of that process is allowing them to make their own decisions and learn from their missteps in order to eventually grow confident in the wisdom of their choices.

Dr. Marcia McNutt is editor in chief of *Science* magazine, the first woman to hold the post in the magazine's 135-year history. She served as director of the US Geological Survey from 2009 to 2013. She began her academic career at Massachusetts Institute of Technology. She is a member of the National Academy of Sciences and was president of the American Geophysical Union from 2000 to 2002.

An Education on the Set

PAMELA FRYMAN

Director-producer

One of the thrills of being a director is the challenge that comes with being part of an incredibly fluid industry. No two days are alike and as the television business changes, we as television directors must learn to grow with it. Every day on set is an education. I have learned to keep my eyes and ears open because you never know who'll be teaching on any particular day. For me, these lessons tend to happen in the moments when I least expect them.

In my professional life, some weeks are by nature more challenging than others. During one such week several years ago, my young twin daughters, Katie and Megan, paid a visit to the set. Seeing their faces across a busy stage always brings a smile to my face. I got quick hugs from them and then turned my attention back to directing the episode while they watched from afar.

I count myself as tremendously lucky to have been able to bring my daughters to the sets of various series and share with them what I believe to be a remarkable example of teamwork. Sitcoms are by nature a collaborative undertaking. If there's an opportunity to improve a joke, you take it. If a piece of furniture gets in the way of some physical comedy, you lose it. If a camera goes down in the middle of a scene, you quickly figure out how to do it with one less. As the director you stand in the middle of it all, filtering and communicating the ideas being thrown at you from all directions. On this particular day, however, the scenes I thought my daughters were seeing were very different from what they were actually watching.

The showrunner of this particular show was a strong-willed man who knew exactly what he wanted, but lacked the ability to let me or anyone else know in a kind way. His voice was consistently a few decibels higher than anyone else's, while his colleagues were utterly silent. The people he was supposed to work with avoided interacting with him at all costs. A great show was produced on that stage, but our days were joyless. At the time, I was unaware of how numb I had become to his behavior toward me and my coworkers. He was disrespectful, inconsiderate, and hostile, and I did not think twice about it. Even more shocking, I took it and allowed it to continue. It took a simple question from one of my daughters to wake me up.

In the car on our way home Megan asked, "Mommy, why do you let that man talk to you that way?" Her straightforward inquiry knocked the wind out of me. Why, indeed? My answer at the time was not memorable, but it's a question I took to heart and needed to answer for myself. The truth was that I knew I was lucky to be on that stage doing that job. But that was by no means a good enough reason to let myself be disrespected by anyone. My daughter knew that I wouldn't have put up with that in any other area of my life, so why should I endure it on the job? I'm on that set, I told myself, because I've worked hard and I'm good at what I do, and I deserve to be there. I have always been sensitive to the treatment of the cast and crew on a stage, but this experience heightened both my awareness and my expectations. Since that time, I've always made it one of my chief responsibilities as a director to establish an atmosphere on the set as one where people want to come to work.

I had the opportunity to work with the same showrunner years later. I walked in with a very different perspective and walked out having had a much more positive experience. I'd like to believe we learned from each other.

There are so many lessons we teach our daughters every single day—by what we say and what we do and how we treat others and how we let them treat us. We lead by example. Not only did my daughter help me realize that I was deserving of much better treatment, but she also reinforced that it is my imperative as a mother to show my daughters that we all have the right to demand to be treated with respect and dignity. The great discovery that I've made as a mother is that as much as I teach my daughters, they teach me more. Lucky me.

Pamela Fryman is a veteran sitcom director who earned two Emmy nominations for her work on the CBS comedy series *How I Met Your Mother*.

Independence

RUTH BADER GINSBURG
Supreme Court justice

I have never thought of myself as a trailblazer. My decision to become a lawyer might have been seen as highly impractical. In the 1950s and '60s, who wanted a lady lawyer?

My daughter, Columbia Law School professor Jane Ginsburg, grew up with two working parents at a time when most mothers did not have jobs outside the home. She saw how her father, Martin Ginsburg, supported me in my teaching and advocacy efforts. He was always in my corner.

My dear Marty was so comfortable with himself that he never regarded me as being any kind of threat. We met when I was seventeen and he was eighteen. I noticed immediately that Marty seemed interested in my conversation and ideas. Most boys at that time didn't care if a girl had a brain—in fact, they preferred that you didn't.

Marty was a fabulous cook. By the time Jane was in high school, she'd noticed a tremendous difference between Mommy's cooking and Daddy's cooking. She phased me out of the kitchen, and Marty became the everyday cook, not just the weekend and company cook.

Jane and her younger brother, James, absorbed the concept of gender equality through the way we lived. It was simply a fact of our lives. I'm very happy that Jane found a husband who is as much a partner to her as Marty was to me. Although in Jane's case, she is the better cook in the family.

My mother, Celia Bader, impressed upon me the importance of being independent. She had been a bookkeeper but stopped working when she married. She and my father later appreciated that her life would have been more satisfying if she had continued working outside the home. Her message to me: while she hoped I would find Prince Charming, I should, in any case, be independent. To her that meant becoming a high school teacher, a job hospitable to women in that era.

My mother was one of the smartest people I ever knew, and a voracious reader. She counseled me always to act like a lady, and to not be distracted by emotions like anger, envy, and resentment. Such feelings sap your energy and waste time. Great counsel that proved to be. My mother died when I was seventeen. Had she lived a long life, I think she would have been enormously pleased with the way things turned out for me.

I attribute my success in law school to my husband and my daughter. Marty and I married the same month I graduated from Cornell University. It was okay for me to follow him to Harvard and study law, friends and relatives thought. Even if no legal employer would take a chance on me, I would still have a man to support me.

Jane was fourteen months old when I started law school. I listened, read, and studied intensively at school until 4 o'clock in the afternoon, then I came home for Jane's time. She was a lively child, and easy to care for. By the time Jane went to sleep for the night, earlier than most children, I was glad to get back to the books.

Jane also made me realize there was more to life than studying hard in law school. I learned this in a devastating way when Jane crawled out of my bedroom with a mouth full of mothballs. She had found them in a bureau drawer where sweaters were stored. We dashed her to Cambridge City Hospital where her stomach was pumped. I recall her screams to this day. Fortunately she had ingested nothing malign.

That experience brought home to me the importance of a multidimensional life. Taking care of Jane and reading to her was fun. Studying law and thinking about legal theory was challenging. I was living two lives, and each one was a respite from the other. Decades later, work-life balance became a topic much talked about. I've often said that I have had it all in my long lifetime, just not all at the same time.

For me, the real eye-opener on the situation for women was Simone de Beauvoir's book *The Second Sex*, which to me was far more stimulating than *The Feminine Mystique*. I never got past the opening chapter of Betty Friedan's book because I never lived the life of a suburban mom.

The time I spent in the early sixties studying and writing about law in Sweden had a profound effect on my career as a law professor, ACLU advocate, federal judge, and finally Supreme Court justice. At the time, 1962 and 1963, women accounted for maybe 3 percent of the law students in the United States. They were already 20 percent of the law students in Sweden. I began to comprehend that an awakening was happening globally about the status of women.

Jane came of age at an energizing time when women were fired up about the possibility of change. She worked as an intern for *Ms. Magazine* in its early days and she earned a master's degree in history. She resisted law school for a while, but I knew it would work for her. Her area of special interest is intellectual property here and abroad. She earned her first law degree from Harvard and her second from the University of Paris.

In Jane's high school yearbook, classmates made predictions about one another's goals in life. Jane's friends wrote that her aspiration was to see her mother appointed to the Supreme Court. And on the next line, they added: "If necessary, Jane will appoint her."

My mother died of cancer the day before I was to graduate from James Madison High School in Brooklyn. Jane and I have experienced her ideal of being successful independent women. The woman who taught me to prize learning would be pleased to know that today my granddaughter, Clara, represents the third generation of women in our family to attend Harvard Law School.

───────

Ruth Bader Ginsburg, nominee of President Clinton, became in 1993 the second woman appointed to the US Supreme Court. As a pioneering advocate for women's rights, she won five of the six gender discrimination cases that she argued before the nation's high court in the 1970s. In 1980, President Carter appointed her to the US Court of Appeals for the District of Columbia. Earlier in her career, from 1963 to 1972, Ginsburg was a professor of law at Rutgers University School of Law. She became the first tenured female professor at Columbia Law School, and taught there from 1972 until 1980. In 1971, she was instrumental in launching the Women's Rights Project of the American Civil Liberties Union. She served as the ACLU's general counsel from 1973 to 1980 and on their national board of directors from 1974 to 1980.

Just a Mom

BROOKE SHIELDS

Actress-author

"Mom, please don't come to the dog park with us."

Those words from my older daughter, Rowan, went through my heart like a knife. I couldn't believe it. Going to the park had always been one of our favorite things to do as a family.

But Rowan had her reasons. She didn't want paparazzi to follow us, which would likely be the case if I came along.

My nine-year-old's anxiety about a simple trip to the park wound up teaching me a lesson and spurring an important conversation for our family about what it means to be famous.

Beyond the practical problems of being hounded by photographers and living in a fishbowl, the influence of celebrity on a young mind can be very corrosive. I've always tried to teach my girls that being famous doesn't make you prettier or smarter or better than other people; it just makes you different.

The focus on fame is part of the reason why my husband and I are raising our daughters in New York City. It's not a one-industry town like Los Angeles. There's greater diversity and less of the feeling that you're only as good as your last project.

Rowan and her younger sister, Grier, have been dealing with the unwelcome side effects of fame ever since they were born, thanks to me. When the issue with the dog park came up, I realized I'd made a big mistake in how I was handling the stress of dealing with aggressive photographers and overzealous fans. I felt bad because I had taught Rowan some important tools for coping with it when she was younger. But after Grier came along, my own fear and anger at having to fend off unwanted attention increased. I felt vulnerable in being responsible for two little girls, and I felt guilty for exposing them to something they'd never asked for.

In the past I had always told Rowan that when people were following us it was important that we hold our heads up high, and to not change the course of our day but just go about our business. I told her what I had learned from others who dealt with the same problem: Don't let yourself become a victim. If you become the hunted, they win. Don't let them make your day on their terms. Don't let them take anything from you emotionally.

I had lived by those rules for years but over time I allowed myself to feel like prey. I'd put the car seat as far back as it would go and try to hide from the cameras as we drove out of our home. I felt an urgency to protect them and frustration that I couldn't give them more of a normal childhood experience. But it turned out that my anxiety about being followed was doing them more harm than good. My husband, writer-producer Chris Henchy, helped me understand this when I was upset over the dog park incident.

I finally took Rowan aside and did what every mother has to do at some point: explain that Mom made a mistake. I hadn't practiced what I preached, and I was making them more scared than we needed to be. And I told her how sad it made me that she didn't want me to come to the park.

Rowan was receptive to my apology—so much so that I realized her drawing the line about the dog park had been a deliberate challenge to me.

The lessons we learned from that incident helped us through another challenging moment where my celebrity impinged on my girls' ability to have a typical preteen experience.

In hindsight, I can't believe I actually agreed to take four girls under the age of ten to see the hottest pop group on the planet—One Direction—at Madison Square Garden. By myself.

My husband teased me a bit for arranging to use the artists' entrance at the Garden in an effort to stay under the radar. Usually I am loath to play the celebrity card to get special privileges. I never try to cut ahead in line just because I happen to be someone a lot of people recognize.

But my daughters' friends only knew me as Mrs. Henchy. I knew it would be weird for them to see people asking me for autographs and pictures.

It wasn't thirty seconds after we got to our seats that people started to come over to me. I didn't even connect the dots until we got inside the Garden that my stint on Disney Channel's *Hannah Montana* (I played her mother) made me just as much a target for One Direction's youthful fans as I was for their parents. At one point Chris Rock spotted me and started calling out "Shields!" I turned around with fire in my eyes and made the knife-across-the-throat gesture. He got the message.

As the gathering around me got bigger, I huddled with the girls and leaned down to look them in the eye. I explained that some people get excited because they've seen me on TV, or because they've read my books, and they just want to say hello. I could tell by the looks on the girls' faces that they were a little rattled.

"I want you all to know something," I said, mustering my confidence as if I were playing a scene. "You are totally safe. And we are going to have fun tonight. I just want you to know that I am totally fine. I want to be nice to these people because they're fans of certain things I've done. But you guys have nothing to worry about."

Fortunately, the house lights went down moments later. For the next two hours, nobody cared about me, it was all about screaming for One Direction. My girls had a good time at the concert just like everyone else.

As much as it's important to protect your physical space, I've also tried to teach my girls how to put the appropriate value on fame and celebrity. It doesn't mean you're better than everyone else or that you command perks and special treatment at every turn.

I was raised with the understanding that the only real value to fame is that it usually helps you to keep working in show business. Who you are as a person—your values, your gifts, your sense of well-being—has nothing to do with how famous you may be.

That message was reinforced to Rowan in a wonderful way

about a month after we had our confrontation over the dog park. Her school hosts a holiday bazaar fund-raiser every year where families shop for gifts at the school, and parents volunteer to wrap them. As I was sitting with other parents manning the wrapping table, Rowan and I both heard very clearly over all the other noise and cross talk a little kid say to his mother: "I know she's been on TV and stuff. But she's really just Rowan's mom. I like to go in her line to have her wrap my presents because she wraps them really well."

I gave Rowan a gentle nudge and a look that said "You see! You see?" That little boy said it better than I ever could.

———

Brooke Shields is an actress and author of the memoirs *There Was a Little Girl: The Real Story of My Mother and Me* and *Down Came the Rain: My Journey Through Postpartum Depression*.

Learning from Tragedy

LAURA W. BUSH

Former first lady

From the time they were tiny babies, I wanted to protect my daughters. I wanted to comfort them if they scraped their knees or if they bruised their hearts. On the terrible morning of 9/11, I made my first telephone calls to them. But sometimes seeing the worst can bring out the very best.

In 2003, my daughter Barbara accompanied George and me to Africa. Experts had been predicting that by 2008, 80 million people would be infected with the AIDS virus. My husband responded by unveiling the President's Emergency Plan for AIDS Relief, the largest international health initiative ever directed at a single disease. PEPFAR committed $15 billion over five years to prevent new infections, to treat those already infected with AIDS, and to care for children orphaned by the loss of a parent to AIDS.

Now, a few months after the announcement, we were going to Africa to see AIDS's devastating toll firsthand. In a pediatric clinic in the nation of Botswana, Barbara and I met a mother who had brought her little girl in for treatment. She had dressed her daughter like an angel, in a lovely lavender-and-white dress to meet the American president. This sweet little child lay on an examining table, so frail and sick. Her mother's last hope was to make her beautiful. At another stop, Barbara became enchanted by a second little girl. The child was eager and curious, but she could barely stand, so she stayed balanced on her mother's lap. Barbara thought she must be a toddler, but she soon learned that this bright-eyed little girl was in fact seven years old. She was just so terribly small and fragile from the ravages of AIDS.

I understood immediately that these mothers were just like me, they wanted to protect their daughters. But until better medicine and medical care could reach them, their precious children were largely beyond protecting. Barbara understood it too. She wanted to find a way to be their comforter and then their protector. But her path was winding, as it almost always is when it ultimately leads to something truly worthwhile.

Barbara went back to school at Yale and enrolled in the university's comprehensive survey course on AIDS, so that she could learn as much about the disease as possible. Then in 2005, after she had graduated, she moved to Cape Town, South Africa, and began working at the Red Cross War Memorial Children's Hospital, which treated a great number of children with AIDS. She was able to help and to provide individual care, but she still yearned for a way to do more.

After South Africa, Barbara moved to New York and took a job at the Cooper Hewitt museum to follow her love of design, but she never stopped thinking of those children—or of how very much they needed. Her answer came at a conference in 2008 hosted by UNAIDS and Google.

Barbara attended, along with her sister, Jenna. During his speech, UNAIDS's CEO Peter Piot challenged the young people in the audience to think of ways that they could help transform global health, ways that they could bring the same remarkable success to the needs of global health that was already being seen in the global fight against AIDS. Barbara, Jenna, and four friends that they had made at the conference began brainstorming and came up with a plan for an organization they would call Global Health Corps. Barbara quit her museum job to help get it launched, and it remains her passion today.

After less than five years, Global Health Corps has sent nearly 300 fellows to five African nations and also to key underserved cities in the United States. The fellows are all recent college graduates and young professionals. They apply their knowledge and creative ideas to do everything, from counseling at-risk teens to helping build medical supply chains, to providing aid to pharmacies in Africa, and to studying health policy for AIDS. Their goal is to improve health care delivery and to make basic health care something that is just as accessible to a mother in Rwanda or Zambia as it is to a mother in Seattle or Fort Lauderdale. And in making health care matter, what matters to them is that this will ultimately save lives.

Barbara comes from a long line of strong women, and a line of women who, sadly, have lost children. My mother-in-law lost her precious little girl, Robin, to leukemia when she was only three years old. My own mother lost three premature babies: two boys and one girl. We are a family that knows the unique pain of losing a child. My daughter wants to make sure that other families are spared that pain, that today's children and their families can have long, healthy, and joyous lives.

What I tell my daughter, both of my daughters, is simply this: you make me proud.

———

Laura W. Bush is both former first lady of the United States and first lady of Texas. A former teacher and librarian, she is a longtime advocate of literacy programs and the health and well-being of women and children.

Letter to My Girls

MONA SINHA

Financial expert—leadership development expert

To my dearest Anya and Riya:

"Be the change you want to see in the world." Mahatma Gandhi's simple words have been my inspiration in life. I hope that as you find yourself on the cusp of adulthood, you, too, will find a simple truth to guide your life choices. I love that you are twins, yet very different human beings. I hope that you will forever treasure the closeness of your unique relationship.

My life as a child was not as simple as yours. I was born the third of three girls in Calcutta. Society at large clucked regretfully as I should have been the much sought-after boy. I grew up with the burden of being the "daughter who should have been the son" and as such felt that I had to fulfill that role. Thankfully, I excelled in school and took on leadership roles, but sometimes it felt like an act to please everyone else around me.

My acceptance into a prestigious college in India was once again proof that I could be as successful as the "boy." However the stifled academic environment and rote learning were huge intellectual disappointments. Furthermore, the murder of Prime Minister Indira Gandhi in 1984 and the subsequent politicization of the campus made learning even more difficult. I decided to take a bold step to leave and attend college in the United States. I decided to apply to women's colleges and when Smith College in Massachusetts admitted me with a full scholarship, I felt truly blessed. I loved the rebellious women that were Smith alumnae—Gloria Steinem to this day is a huge role model. It was at Smith, free from expectations of parents and society, that I was able to explore, take risks, and discover my authentic self. It was at Smith that I finally proved that you didn't need to be a boy to make a difference.

Smith allowed me to be genuine—to find innovative solutions to problems that were difficult, to discover who I really was, to find my voice. I had to speak up when I was not awarded enough financial aid in my sophomore year. On another occasion, I had to find a way to get into a program in Washington, DC, that had never hosted a scholarship-supported international student. I also had to interpret the *Bhagavad Gita* for a friend who asked me about Hinduism in a way that I had never before considered. These are the experiences that freed me and made me determined to allow you, my girls, to shine in any way that you please as you find your passion for life. Anya, I can see how your compassion for others will take you far. Riya, I see how your grit and determination, displayed so vividly on the soccer field, will motivate you to push forward. Keep these qualities and develop them further as they will help shape you.

My decision postcollege to pursue investment banking was an extension of my confidence in my ability to compete in a largely male-dominated world. At Smith, I had been told that I could do anything, encouraged by the many female role models (professors, advisors, staff, and alumnae) who supported me and pushed me. As I began my first job on Wall Street, I realized that gender equality was great in theory but not really played out in practice. I learned a tremendous amount and enjoyed working in the intense atmosphere of mergers and acquisitions, but faced sexist comments and was often solicited to engage improperly. It was hard and often with a thumping heart that I had to stand my ground with some pretty influential men, but in the long run it stood me in good stead. My belief in myself and my determination to be true to my own values enabled me to earn respect. I did not play the game. That in a nutshell is the most important lesson of leadership and life.

As I have transitioned from working on Wall Street to restructuring businesses in Asia to finally dedicating myself to investing in women's education and development as leaders and entrepreneurs, I have learned that being authentic and understanding a few simple truths are the tenets of a successful life.

- Technology will give you many tools but may hamper your creativity and ability to think out of the box.
- Be careful not to limit yourself to easy answers. Take risks and know that it's okay to fail sometimes.
- Fear is not a reason to not do something.
- Use love and compassion even when all else fails.

- Respect the choices that people make, especially if they diverge widely from your own. When you respect others fully, only then will you be respected back.

You often ask why we have so many young women stay at our house—sometimes for a few days, sometimes for an entire summer. These are my mentees—girls and women that I advise and support as I see the sparkle within them that they have yet to discover themselves. My greatest joy is to see my mentees fly and achieve something that they thought was impossible for them to do. I want to be their safety net as I am yours. I want to be their rock as I have so hugely benefitted from my own rock of family—your dad, your brother, and you two.

I hope you live a life that is whole. I hope you find joy, every day, in things both big and small. Live a life of excellence, as defined by your own expectation of what that means. Build a life that cherishes the lessons of the past to reap the dreams of the future. Fill your life with compassion, determination, grit, and strength of character to ease the world of its many worries.

I regret that I won't be there to see your lives completely lived. But I hope that the lessons I teach you from my life bring to you something to use in your own. I hope you enjoy many moments of happiness and feel the thrill of changing something that is wrong. Make the right choices for yourselves and know that I love you and will always remain your biggest supporter.

Mona Sinha is a founder of the project to establish the Asian Women's Leadership University in Malaysia. She is also an advisor and director of Impact Investment Exchange Asia, the first social stock exchange being set up in Singapore. She began her professional career as an investment banker at Morgan Stanley, followed by a marketing career at Procter & Gamble and Unilever. In 2010, she worked on a project for Goldman Sachs Asia on the development of Asian leadership. She holds an MBA from Columbia University and serves as an advisory director to the Columbia Business School Social Enterprise program. She is a trustee of Smith College.

Don't Agonize, Organize

GLORIA ALLRED
Attorney-activist

My daughter, Lisa Bloom, is often asked what it was like to grow up with me as her mother. I am thrilled to say that she usually answers this question with one word: empowering.

Long before I began making headlines as an attorney representing high-profile cases, I was keenly aware of the need to help my daughter understand the importance of fighting for what was right, and what was fair, especially as it involved discrimination against women and girls.

When Lisa was in the fourth grade, she was once told that she couldn't participate in square dancing because she was wearing pants rather than a skirt. It was bad enough that it was the 1970s and her public school had only recently allowed girls to wear pants. Lisa told me at dinner that she had cried at her desk that day because the teacher wouldn't let her square-dance.

The two of us marched into the principal's office the next day. I explained how this rule, apparently made up on the spot by the teacher, was unfair to girls. The man gave me a strange look as I made my case, but when I finished talking, there was no more rule.

Lisa has said that this victory made a big impression on her. As a mother, I was motivated to respond to her hurt feelings, but I also wanted to demonstrate that we all have the ability to question and confront authority. The square-dancing dustup was an opportunity to teach by example one of my guiding principles: When you want something, and someone in power says no, that's just the beginning of the conversation.

A few years later another opportunity to challenge a policy that discriminated against girls arose when some of Lisa's girlfriends were upset by the school's tradition of limiting the annual faculty-student softball game to boys only. Although Lisa had no interest in playing softball, she followed my motherly advice: "Don't agonize, organize." That was a quote from the famous labor organizer Mother Jones that I often repeated.

I was proud when my sixth grader took a leading role in organizing a group that held a rally, chanted feminist slogans, and ultimately won their fight to make it a coed game.

There were times when Lisa was a little embarrassed by my crusading nature, like when I grilled a teacher at Back-to-School Night about the lack of information about women and minorities in her history textbook, or when I pushed the school for details on whether girls' sports programs received as much funding as the programs for the boys. However, I knew I was teaching my daughter important lessons about standing up for equality, and that girls should enjoy equal opportunities with boys.

I knew I was raising a formidable child when Lisa began collecting buttons and bumper stickers with feminist slogans. Her favorite: WOMEN WHO SEEK TO BE EQUAL TO MEN LACK AMBITION.

I encouraged her to go to law school and was gratified when she flourished at Yale. She has an impressive career as a lawyer, an author, and a legal commentator on NBC's *Today* show. She is also a wonderful mother to my grandchildren, Sarah and Sam.

As much as I focused on guiding Lisa to become a lawyer and assist women and minorities as I do, I also wanted her to understand the importance of being her own person, and make her own choices. I have a sign in my office that reads: BE REASONABLE. DO IT MY WAY—but that didn't always apply for Lisa.

I tried most of all to let her know that I loved her for who she was, and that she had the right to live her life and to have her own aspirations even though they might be different from mine.

I cheered from afar when Lisa decided to climb Kilimanjaro even though it was something I would never do. I supported her when she took an interest in martial arts even though I wasn't crazy about the idea. In addition to her right to the pursuit of happiness, I also wanted Lisa to learn certain values and that she owed a duty not only to her family, but also to the world to help others and make it a better place.

Lisa has told me that she recognizes the debt that her generation owes to mine in breaking down barriers for women in all aspects of society. She had a front-row seat to many of the defining battles of our times. She saw me take on cases and causes that I believe in—in order to win justice.

In her work as a lawyer and as a mother, Lisa reflects everything I had hoped for, and so much more. When I think about her, I always remind myself that I'm fighting to make the world a better place, a more equitable place, not just for Lisa but for everyone's daughters.

————

Gloria Allred is a Los Angeles attorney and partner in the law firm of Allred Maroko & Goldberg. She is also the author of *Fight Back and Win: My Thirty-Year Fight Against Injustice—And How You Can Win Your Own Battles.*

Thelma, Eva, and Me

JOY MARCUS
Media executive—entrepreneur

What have I told my daughter? It started with making sure Eva understood the lineage of strong women in our family.

My mother did not graduate from college and did not have a traditional career, but she was full of grit. She believed strongly in women and their ability to succeed.

Thelma was born on the Lower East Side of Manhattan to a close-knit Jewish family. Her father left a budding business in Warsaw to make his way in the United States, landing first in the tenements of Orchard Street and eventually moving to a largish East Village apartment where my mother spent her first thirty-nine years.

My mother was raised by her parents, and also by a group of aunts and uncles who lived within four blocks of one another. There were twelve cousins altogether. According to the family, my mother was the smart, stylish one. She was the only one who went to college, spending two years at Brooklyn College as a math major.

She left college to help her ailing father with his retail business. Around this time she married and gave birth to my sister, Claire. Grandpa Sam died the day after Claire was born. We will never know the true story—it got lost with a generation—but family legend has it that my mother "threw out" Claire's father shortly thereafter. The family sent Mom and Claire to Miami for a year to take advantage of Florida's looser divorce laws. We have many pictures of them from that time lying in the sun by swimming pools at Art Deco hotels. They look gorgeous and happy.

Gussie and my mother's sister Beatrice then threw themselves into raising Claire with my mom. Claire was a brilliant student. In their eyes she could do anything.

Thelma met Ruby, my father, when Claire was ten. He was a Polish immigrant just like her father, a refugee from the Nazis, with little family of his own in the United States. But like Sam he had started a successful business. The family cautiously embraced him and he embraced Claire. He and Thelma married and then I came along. Ruby adopted Claire and we all shared the same last name.

Thelma and Ruby always believed that their girls could do anything. Astronaut? Check. Talmud teacher? Check. President of the United States? Check. There were simply no boundaries to their belief in us and we felt it every day. I went to Princeton University not long after they started admitting women. It never occurred to me that I was being bold until they gave us a T-shirt on my first day that read "Glad to be here—too bad it took 200 years."

My mother's advice was to be as smart as I could be about whatever interested me. And she told me not to learn how to type because she worried I would end up a secretary. That was the only practical career advice she ever gave me.

When I married the wrong person, Thelma challenged me up to the day of the wedding (a fancy one-per-family tradition). When I decided to get out of the marriage, she was already ill but showed up at my apartment with her nurse to help me move my ex-husband's stuff out.

When I met my husband, David, she was quite ill. But she knew right away. An Oberlin English major via Cornell Law School who wanted a nontraditional legal career. She knew this meant that I would be the main breadwinner in the family. She didn't care a bit. She loved David from the moment she met him and knew that he would support me in fulfilling my dreams.

And then came Ethan, the first love of our lives. And then Eva. Born in 2000, my daughter has so much of my mother in her, particularly her gorgeous eyes and determination. But she is taller and far more athletic than any of us Zimelman women. And she has my mother's style gene.

Most of what I've tried to teach Eva has been done with actions and not words. It starts with the things that I did not do. I did not stay home very long after she was born. I left her in the care of her father, who had a more flexible academic schedule, and some au pairs.

At Eva's Manhattan private schools, David was almost always the only dad at drop-off and pickup times. He scheduled the play dates and went to the park and took her to those sometimes horrific birthday parties. This was normal to Eva, as it had been to Ethan. My kids saw through our actions that parenting is a partnership and that moms don't always come through with bake sale duty.

And then there is what I did.

I was present, physically and emotionally present, whenever conceivably possible. Home for dinner at least three nights during the workweek unless I had to travel. Always home for Shabbat dinner on Friday night. I would put together bags of snacks at six a.m. because I wanted to be part of her day. I physically ached to be part of her life. I told her constantly that I loved her unconditionally and that she was the most important thing in my life, no matter what. When I really wanted to get her attention, I would tell her simply: "I would take a bullet for you."

Eva and her brother grew up watching me fiercely pursue career goals. Just as Eva was old enough to appreciate how much work it entailed, I hit the three-job trifecta moment of being a partner in a venture firm, the CEO of a start-up, and a professor at Princeton University. I have been open with her about how hard some of it has been and how gratifying and fun it can be, most of the time.

Now that she is a teenager we speak more directly. She asks questions that scare me. She asks about sexual consent at high school parties and on college campuses (she started a meme on Facebook #bringconsentbacktocollege during her freshman year). She asks about double standards in school dress code—why is it not okay for a girl to show off her body?

I answer these questions as best I can. I want her to be safe above all else and at the same time feel no boundaries. So far, she excels at sports, she's in honors classes by choice, and she regularly speaks in front of the entire student body through her role in student government. I think it's working.

Eva seeks ways to encourage the feminist conversation at school but is vehemently feminine in her appearance and demeanor. She goes on dates and expresses her desire to eventually marry and have children. And she has every expectation that her life partner will support her in everything she does. Because that's what husbands and wives do in our family. Thelma would approve.

Joy Marcus is executive vice president and general manager of the digital video network of Condé Nast Entertainment. She is an Internet media veteran and has both run and invested in digital media start-ups. Marcus founded the French video site Dailymotion's business in the United States and sold the company to telecom powerhouse Orange in 2011. She was a managing director at Gotham Ventures, Draper Fisher Jurvetson's New York fund, where she focused on investments in female-led start-ups, including DailyWorth, now Worth.fm. Marcus also served as a James Wei Visiting Professor at Princeton University, where she taught entrepreneurship in the spring of 2015.

The Gift of Getting Fired

JUDY VREDENBURGH

Nonprofit executive

I was always the moneymaker in our family. My husband, a professor, has good ideas and many insights, but my drive to achieve in business enabled us to live comfortably on the Upper East Side in New York City.

I worked in retail merchandising right out of college. I had the combination of motivation, analytical ability, negotiation savvy, and determination that enabled me to gain increasingly more responsibility and commensurate compensation.

I worked hard and earned promotions, advancing to merchandise vice president. And then I had to leave a company I loved in order to gain the next position, one that was always held at that time by a man. I became a senior vice president and general merchandise manager. Ultimately, I secured a CEO opportunity at yet another retailer.

And then, after only one year, my corporate boss and I disagreed on the strategic direction for the company. I was fired. What seemed like a career setback turned out to be a teachable moment, and a wonderful gift for me and for my daughter.

Our only child, Cynthia, was involved in staging a middle-school play at the time. Because my demanding career had prevented me from participating much in Cynthia's school life, beyond parent-teacher conferences and viewing an occasional sporting event, I quickly decided to use my sudden free time as a volunteer for this most important production of the musical *Once Upon a Mattress*.

I helped with whatever was needed, including working with another volunteer to create all the costumes. Cynthia was happy to have me visibly involved for the first time at her school. We shared a lot of time together at home, while I searched for a job, and we talked. I explained to her that I had not failed, but that my boss became impatient after a short period of time while I was experimenting with a different strategic direction. I told her I felt sad about being fired but that that act did not alter who I was or what I had accomplished in my career. I indicated that I was not going to let that event lessen my confidence and ambition and described how sometimes events happen that are uncontrollable.

While investigating positions in retail merchandising, my long-felt desire to work on behalf of social good increasingly asserted itself and I switched my employment search to the nonprofit sector. When this resulted in an excellent national position at a prestigious nonprofit organization, March of Dimes, my husband communicated to Cynthia that her mother had planned as an undergraduate to first work in the profit sector to build economic assets and then move to the nonprofit sector to contribute to the social good. I made it clear to her that I was emphasizing values other than high income.

An important part of this learning experience for Cynthia was the observation of what happens with significant change. She became reassured when she witnessed firsthand my reaction and is today a reasonable risk taker. I demonstrated through discussion and calmness that I viewed my circumstance, after initial hurt, as an opportunity. This reassured her that I was all right and our family was not threatened. I credit the influence of my parents, who raised me with both high performance expectations and with unconditional love and support, for allowing me to field this career curveball with calm and confidence.

Today Cynthia is a highly successful marketer and business developer, wife, and mother of a baby daughter. Over the years we have referred to this incident and found it helpful. Experiencing setbacks and obstacles at work occurs frequently, and one's reaction to them is often more important than the original cause. When Cynthia confronts significant work problems now, I sometimes remind her of my firing and try to help her gain perspective. I communicate that with each obstacle comes opportunity if you believe in and know yourself, learn from each situation, and remember to have perspective about what's really important in the long run.

My daughter and I will never forget the fun and fulfillment we both experienced by being so intimately involved with that production of *Once Upon a Mattress*. Some teachable moments last a lifetime.

———

Judy Vredenburgh has been president and CEO of Girls Inc. since 2010. She has served on President Obama's Advisory Council of Faith-Based and Neighborhood Partnerships. She previously served as president and CEO of Big Brothers Big Sisters of America and was a senior vice president at the March of Dimes Birth Defects Foundation.

Privileges

SHARON OSBOURNE
Music manager—TV personality

My daughters, you were born into a life of privilege but it wasn't a storybook upbringing.

I did not have the luxury of being a stay-at-home mum. I worked, which meant a lot of travel, which must have been very disruptive to you and your brother, seeing both of your parents come and go while you were left with nannies.

I want you to know it was devastating for me. If I could do it all over again I would never have worked while you were growing up.

Your childhood flew by for me. I woke up one day and you were both fully grown. There were so many times when I just wanted to be a regular stay-at-home mum. But truthfully I don't think that would have really been me.

It's a gift to have the time to raise your own children. Aimee and Kelly, I want you to never forget that when it comes time to bring your own children into the world.

Although we were apart sometimes, I worked hard to instill a moral code for you both. I wanted you to live by high standards, never have a sense of entitlement, not judge others, be accepting, tolerant, and always open-minded. And on that, you've never let me down.

I want you both to know that whatever your father's done and whatever I've done in our lives has nothing to do with you—good or bad. The most important thing I can tell you both is to be good, be respectful, and be honest. And I also want you to realize it's very important to find your passion in life, and follow it. Whatever it is, you should have a passion for what you do. In life, there will always be somebody richer, prettier, younger, and more talented than you, but life is not a competition.

We are all so different and unique and that is what makes us all special. There is nobody in the world like you both nor anybody who has had your life experiences, and that is what you should embrace—your individuality. Stand up for what you believe in, live your life, don't waste it, realize you are healthy, loved, and are free young women with a voice, use it.

Aimee showed me how well she'd learned that lesson when she was sixteen and our family had the amazing experience of doing *The Osbournes* TV show for MTV. It was supposed to only be for three weeks, but after Aimee learned what would be expected of her, she said "I'm bailing on this" and went to live in the guesthouse. She just decided it wasn't for her. She didn't want that invasion in her life.

I was proud of Aimee for knowing what she wanted, but I was frustrated that my daughter didn't go on that great ride with us. We were so shocked by the reaction to the show—all of a sudden one day we were known by the whole world. And I wanted us all to be together in it. I had to adapt my thinking in hindsight with the understanding that she did the right thing for her at the time. Aimee likes to sing and she writes music, but she's never fought to be famous.

Even after *The Osbournes* took off, I told Kelly and Jack, "Enjoy every moment because it's a ride, and the ride always comes to an end." I told them in no uncertain terms, "This will not last." The money, the fame will eventually end and there'll be somebody new who's on the ride.

It's important to know "this too will pass" even while you're in the thick of it so you know to just enjoy it and don't waste the opportunity. Because none of it's real. None of it is permanent. All you can do is hope you have a good reputation and a good work ethic, and hope that as one door closes another opens.

Aimee and Kelly, I want you both to know how proud I am of you. I'm proud of you as people for being strong and grounded and having a good moral code that you both live by. Whatever you have achieved in life you've done through your own hard work.

I love and admire you both, and I hope you know that you are both the light of my life.

Please hurry up and have babies because I need more grandchildren.

Love,
Mama

———————

Sharon Osbourne is a cohost of the CBS daytime series *The Talk* and a judge on the UK edition of *The X Factor*. She won an Emmy for the groundbreaking MTV reality series *The Osbournes*.

Women Have a Voice

BEVERLY JOHNSON

Model-entrepreneur

My daughter was almost eighteen when she came to me with the words I'd hoped to never hear from her. She and a friend had decided to move to New York to break into modeling.

"Mom, this is something I have to do," Anansa told me. Of course, she wanted no help from me. She wanted to do it all on her own. She was bold. I was terrified.

After about six months, I started to hear reports from agents and photographers. Anansa definitely had people interested in working with her. I started to warm up to the idea of her going into the business that made me famous, even though I knew what a hard road lay ahead for my beautiful girl.

Then one day I got a phone call.

"Mom, guess what?"

"You're pregnant?"

"No, no, no," Anansa said in exasperation. "I don't want to be a model anymore."

Her explanation reminded me why I was so nervous about her trying modeling in the first place. She was starving herself all the time to lose weight. She'd fainted on the way to an audition. She'd been stood up by photographers who promised to meet with her. And her agent kept pressing her to lose "just five more pounds." At this point, Anansa hit her limit.

"Mom, I will never let anyone else tell me how I should look, ever again."

I was blown away. It took me forty years to reach this understanding about myself. Anansa got there in less than a year.

She came back home to Los Angeles to live with me and then go to school. She earned a BA in business with a minor in economics in just two and a half years from Buffalo State College, and an MBA from Trinity College. I hoped she would try law school, something I had aspired to in my college years. But one day while I was working on the TVLand reality show *She's Got the Look*, I got a phone call.

"Mom, guess what?"

"You're pregnant?"

"No! Why do you always lead with that?"

Anansa's news this time was that she had been approached to work as a plus-size model. I was surprised at first. She's a size 10 or so—a perfectly normal figure for a healthy woman. I wanted to know her reasoning.

"I think I can be a role model for women to love themselves exactly as they are—who they are and how they look," Anansa told me.

All I could think was, "Whoa. I raised *this* girl?" Anansa went on to become one of the top 10 plus-size models in the world.

Anansa forged her own path to success just as I did after she was born in 1978. I was twenty-six and at the top of my game. But models simply did not have children back then. It meant the end of your career. As a model in those days, you could only count on working steadily for about five or six years, anyway, before your run was over.

But for me, the birth of Anansa marked the beginning of my second career. I didn't want to retire. I was lucky to be able to reinvent myself by writing beauty books, producing a television show, acting, singing, and branding and licensing my name for a line of wigs and hair-care products. I always saw "Beverly Johnson" as being the foundation of a business, not just a face on magazine covers.

My daughter and I have become so much closer now that she is a mother and businesswoman herself. When Anansa was growing up our lives were rocked by a horrific custody battle that played out between her father and me. He won primary custody until she was eleven, when she finally told him she wanted to live with me. It was a difficult power struggle for years. When Anansa came back to me, I had her read the court transcripts of the custody battle. I wanted her to see it in black and white so she would know why she had been living with her father. I tried to instill in her the kind of strength that I had achieved with the help of my mother after facing difficult challenges in my life.

After Anansa had been married for a year, I got the call that I had anticipated for so long—finally she was pregnant!—and

I was overjoyed. As she prepared to give birth we reexamined our relationship. Parts of that process were very painful. When she looked at me with her baby daughter, Ava, in her arms and said, "I can't imagine the pain you went through when you lost custody of me," I felt like screaming, "She got it!"

As an adult, a turning point in Anansa's life came when she stood up to her father about her choice of a husband. I had my doubts about him, too, but Anansa knew what she was doing. David has become the son I always wanted. They have given me two more grandchildren, both boys. The fullness of our family life led us to produce *Beverly's Full House* for the Oprah Winfrey Network. It was one of the highest-rated shows on the network.

Working as a model forced me to grow up very fast in the face of incredible pressure and life-threatening situations. But in other ways, I was slow to mature. I made mistakes. In time I used the strength that I gained from my mother to find my way. I felt the weight of experiencing a full-circle moment when I saw the lightbulb go off in Anansa's mind after she had given birth to her own daughter. I always told her that "women have a voice" no matter what the situation. As mothers, it's our responsibility to pass the torch.

Beverly Johnson made fashion history in 1974 when she became the first African-American model featured on the cover of *Vogue*. After establishing herself as a pioneering supermodel, Johnson branched out into acting and singing as well as launching several businesses, including a line of hair-care products and wigs. She starred in and produced the 2012 OWN documentary series *Beverly's Full House*. She is the author of the *New York Times* best-selling memoir *The Face That Changed It All*. In 1993, the *New York Times* named Johnson one of the twentieth century's fifty most influential people in fashion.

Simply Irresistible

MICHELLE KING

Writer-producer

I like to think I'm teaching my teenage daughter, Sophia, to be a strong, self-confident feminist, but it's possible I'm just teaching her to fear my driving.

Heading to the airport in rush-hour traffic, we heard a radio broadcast about a recent Iowa Supreme Court decision. In Fort Dodge, Iowa, a male dentist had fired his female dental assistant simply because he found her "irresistible." The woman had been working there for ten years, and even the dentist admitted she was extremely qualified—that she'd done nothing wrong and was the best assistant he'd ever had.

There was no evidence of flirtatious behavior on her part. She never did anything to encourage his sexual advances. Instead, the dentist claimed that because his assistant was so attractive, he was afraid he might try to start an affair with her.

The broadcast went on to report that the dental assistant—who was also married and had two small children—brought suit and a lower court sided with the dentist. So the dental assistant took the case to the Iowa State Supreme Court—the all-male Iowa State Supreme Court.

According to the Iowa Supreme Court, the dental assistant's firing didn't violate the state's Civil Rights Act. It wasn't sexual discrimination. The court decided that the assistant wasn't fired because of her gender, but because the dentist considered her a threat to his marriage. She was just too pretty. There was nothing illegal about it.

I turned up the radio and turned up my voice. "Are you hearing this?!" I demanded of Sophia. "Forget that the assistant was extremely competent!! Forget that the dentist was the one that created the problem! The dentist chose to fire her because of her looks, and a State Supreme Court—an all-male State Supreme Court—thought that was totally and completely fine!!!"

I looked over and Sophia appeared horrified.

Rigid. Speechless.

Maybe it was the injustice. Or maybe it was because I was swerving toward oncoming traffic.

But I wasn't even close to finished. There were steering wheels to be pounded. There were expletives to be shouted. Multisyllabic expletives.

"Do you understand how unfair this is?! A guy can actually get away with firing a totally competent woman just because he wants to sleep with her! You realize that all your friends should be going to law school! This is why we need women on every single Supreme Court!!!!!"

Sophia nodded vigorously. "Oh, yeah, totally. Women on every Supreme Court."

Anything to get me refocused on the truck heading toward us.

But as with so many things, Sophia was the one to do the actual teaching.

The next day she told me the story of the boy who sits behind her in homeroom. He'd always been kind of a jerk, interrupting the teacher, talking a lot in class—but then he stole a box of Girl Scout cookies that Sophia had bought to support a friend. Sophia asked the boy to return them, but he just walked away and started eating them.

So Sophia charged after the boy, smacked him on the back of the head, and grabbed her cookies.

I resisted the urge to ask my real question—"You hit someone?!"—and went for the more neutral, "Then what happened?"

Sophia answered casually, "Nothing. That was about a month ago, and he *never* bothers me anymore."

So what I learned is this: We need smart, clear-eyed female judges. But we also need tough, self-confident young women willing to smack the bullies when they get out of hand.

And I think Sophia learned to keep CDs in the car.

Michelle King is an Emmy-nominated writer and producer. She is the cocreator and executive producer of the CBS drama *The Good Wife*.

Not Much

KAREN ANTMAN, MD

Physician-academic

When considering the question of what I told my daughter, my first thought was "Not much." Amy was seriously independent from the time she was a toddler. At the age of four, she did not hesitate to give back a present from a male relative when he insisted she give him a kiss in exchange. Other relatives tried to get me to convince her to kiss him, but I supported her reaction.

My husband and I met while in medical school at Columbia University. Amy was born at Columbia University Medical Center during the last year of our internal medicine residency. Later, we both joined the faculty of Harvard Medical School. Elliott directed the coronary care unit, and I directed a bone marrow transplant program. Our workdays were long and demanding. The lessons we imparted to Amy and her younger brother, David, usually came in the form of stories, many of which were shared through animated and highly opinionated conversations at the dinner table.

Amy and David particularly enjoyed the true story of the hospital staff member who, during a Code Blue emergency, tried to move a stuffed chair to make room for the arriving cardiac arrest team. He only succeeded in wedging it into the doorway, which then required each arrest team member to climb over the chair to get into the room—a great example of unintended consequences and flawed planning. There was also the story of the mother and eighteen-year-old daughter. The daughter complained of crampy abdominal pain but denied in front of her mother that she could possibly be pregnant. Ten minutes after she was sent to the restroom for a urine sample, obstetrics and pediatrics were paged to the ER ladies' room. Clearly, don't rely completely on everything people tell you, particularly when they may be motivated to be less than totally forthcoming.

Presenting research findings at meetings was also an important part of academic life. To avoid absences from the kids for days at a time, we regularly took them with us to medical meetings all over the world. Our children saw the Great Wall of China, ate chocolate croissants in Paris, and thoroughly enjoyed the animals in Australia. I was often amazed at the differences between Amy and David's experiences and my own childhood growing up on a farm in rural Pennsylvania.

By the time they got to high school we told our kids that as long as they made good decisions we would not interfere. We assured them that if they called us in a time of need, we would come get them anywhere, anytime, no questions asked. As physicians we were early adopters of cell phones, then big and clunky. We begged Amy to take one on dates but she refused since none of her friends had them.

Amy maintained an impressive level of self-confidence and determination through her teenage years. The only way we knew which colleges she applied for was because we had to write the checks. We never did see her application essay. I trusted that she would find the right path without pushing or prodding from me.

In college, Amy changed majors every couple of months, clearly curious about a variety of disciplines. I spent an entire family wedding keeping her grandfather from voicing his objections to her latest goal of being a chef. A few months later she settled on another major, interplanetary geology. But after a summer internship studying imaging data from a NASA mission, she returned home saying, "I can't live my life in front of a monitor" and started taking premed requirements. We privately smiled but said nothing.

During Amy's first year of medical school, she brought home our son-in-law-to-be, Jeff. We tried not to comment on how much we liked him out of fear our approval might get this wonderful young man fired. Fortunately she came to the same conclusion about him that we did.

Amy became a pediatric neurologist and is now on the faculty of the University of California, San Francisco. Like her parents, she is living a life of academics, medicine, and parenting. For my daughter, engaging stories and many good role models of people who loved their work helped set her on a path to happiness and fulfillment. But let's hear her side of this story.

———————

Dr. Karen Antman is dean of Boston University's School of Medicine and an internationally recognized expert on breast cancer, mesotheliomas, and sarcomas. She was previously deputy director for Translational and Clinical Sciences at the National Cancer Institute as well as the Wu Professor of Medicine and Pharmacology and Director of the Herbert Irving Comprehensive Cancer Center at Columbia University College of Physicians and Surgeons. She served on the faculty of Harvard Medical School from 1979 to 1993.

So Much

AMY ANTMAN GELFAND, MD

Physician-academic

One of the most endearing qualities of my mother and father during my childhood was how they hesitated to lecture or impose unsolicited opinions on me. They were always there to provide perspective on a situation, but only when asked. "Not much" was also what I thought when asked to remember specific life lessons articulated by my mother. Instead, I learned so much from all the things my mother did, rather than said.

It was obvious my mother loved being a doctor. She worked hard, but with such curiosity and motivation to improve medicine that most of the time it didn't look like work. She was always eager to exchange ideas about science and biology at the dinner table, with anyone, anytime. She found meaning in medicine. I knew this from the stories she shared.

I remember the day my mother came home and told us

about a breast cancer patient of hers who had reached the all-important milestone of five years in remission. My mother wrote out a prescription for a nice dinner with a good bottle of wine and then handed it to the woman's husband to be filled. What little girl wouldn't want to be a doctor? You get to make people better.

One thing I do recall my mother explicitly advising me during adolescence was that "choosing who you marry is one of the most important decisions you will ever make in your life." This has turned out to be tremendously good advice.

In a stroke of phenomenal luck, I managed to marry the kindest, smartest person I have ever met. My husband, also a neurologist, not only supports but helps to expand my ambitious career agenda. And we have enlarged our family to include three beautiful children.

So what will I tell my own daughter, Abigail, who is not quite five months old as I write this? Not much, I hope. Just plenty of stories.

––––––––––

Dr. Amy Antman Gelfand is a child neurologist at the University of California, San Francisco Headache Center. A graduate of Harvard Medical School, Gelfand specializes in diagnosing and treating children who suffer from a variety of headache disorders. She is a member of the American Academy of Neurology, the Child Neurology Society, and the American Headache Society.

My Mother's Example

MARY STEENBURGEN

Actress—environmental activist

My mother was an ardent feminist. She never marched in a rally or wore a button or had bumper stickers on her car. She never yelled at anyone about it or embarrassed those who felt differently than she did. She never read a book about feminist values. She just lived them. To her, it was about fairness—that obvious and therefore often overlooked principle that should be the foundation of any desire for change. My mom just thought that life should be fair for everyone.

When I was eight, I watched my feminist mother go to work to support our family without batting an eye. I grew up in North Little Rock, Arkansas. My father, a train conductor, couldn't work for much of my childhood due to heart problems. My mother pitched in and worked a nine-to-five job as a secretary. To this day, my sister and I marvel at how she could work all day, and still put a hot meal on the table for us after she got home. And she also found the time to make most of our clothes.

I realize now that she must have been tired, fed up, and scared many of those nights, but I hardly ever saw her express those feelings while I was growing up. Everything that is resonant with me about feminism came from watching her in those days. Without ever hearing her say it, I learned from her example that a woman could do just about anything and, most importantly, rise to the occasion when the going got tough. I learned from her that it was possible to be a great mother and a breadwinner at the same time. It wasn't easy, but it was possible.

I love that my work causes me to meet so many young people. But I am astounded by the young women I've met who say, "I'm ambitious but, I mean, I'm not a feminist or anything . . ." I always gently reply, "But you don't want to do your best in life? To dream your dreams and work to achieve them? And do you not want to be treated fairly? By your employers and coworkers and in all your relationships?" The answer is, usually, "Of course."

That's all that being a feminist is. You can dress it up or tear it down and bumper-sticker the hell out of it, but that's all it is. It harkens back to my mother's fundamental concept of fairness. I want to live the very fullest life I can. I want to challenge myself. I want to grow and try new things up to my last breath. I want to love my family *and* my career. And I want that potential for any chosen path to be available to every young person in the world. For many young women, that path is mountainous. I especially want it for them. Again, to me, that is feminism.

I hope that our three daughters have learned something

from me about saying yes to opportunities in life. I hope that I have encouraged them to listen to their heart's desire. I have never lied to them about how hard it is to "have it all" at times. For all of my accomplishments, they know that being a mother and stepmother has been my most thrilling adventure—and in no way at odds with being a feminist. They are very grateful for life's blessings and I have watched them work with young people, giving back to their communities. Now that they are adults, I watch them on their journeys with wonder and pride. They don't hide their intelligence away. They don't hide their strength away. They have already weathered some tough storms, just as I had by their age, but those storms have served to deepen their experience of life and of what it is to be a woman.

I am living in the midst of the very special privilege of being a grandparent. It is, indeed, grand. Beyond the mind-boggling love that I feel for my granddaughters, the most beautiful thing of all is watching my daughter and her husband shine as parents. They may not always feel very shiny at the end of a long day, but they are. The respect that they give each other and their children is a thrilling thing for me to watch.

My girls have grown up surrounded by my favorite kind of men—those who delight in women being the best they can be, and those whose sense of manhood is not predicated on tearing anyone else down.

My hope is that someday we won't need the label of "feminist" for a woman who seeks fairness, for herself and for all women. I think all labels for people are inherently divisive. Men don't have to wear such a label, and I wouldn't wish it on my son or husband.

But until then, I am a proud feminist. Just like Nell Steenburgen, I can't imagine wanting anything less for myself, or my daughters and granddaughters.

————

Mary Steenburgen is an Oscar-winning actress and environmental activist.

Color-Blind Lenses

KIMBERLEY HATCHETT

Financial advisor—youth mentor

My daughter, Lauren, is a miracle baby.

My chances of having a child in my late thirties were written off by so many doctors. I went through twenty-two intrauterine-insemination procedures and ten in vitro fertilization procedures, to no avail. I finally started getting kicked out of fertility clinics because I was told I would bring their success ratio down.

By the time my husband and I decided we would adopt a child—right when I gave it back to the universe—my daughter came along, naturally. From the moment she was born, she was this sassy little girl. My one and only.

Having a daughter was so perfect for me, because over the course of my career as a wealth management advisor I have invested a lot of time in mentoring and advising young girls on how to succeed, how to become leaders, and how to be fearless in the pursuit of their dreams.

I tell them stories about my upbringing, in one of the very few African-American families living in Lawrenceville, New Jersey, in the 1970s, and how I built my career as a financial advisor at Morgan Stanley. Very few of my clients look like me—95 percent of them are white men—but I have thrived in this field because I love what I do and I'm good at connecting with people.

I learned from my father the importance of looking at the world through "color-blind lenses." He would always tell me that in this world there's no black, there's no white, there's just shades of gray. There are just people.

William Hatchett—everyone called him Bucky—was a force of nature. He was an all-American in football, basketball, and track and field in college. He was the first African-American president of the student body at his high school in Verona, New Jersey, when the school was 99 percent white, and he was also the first black president of the student body at Rutgers University.

My father had a powerful experience while on the basketball team at Rutgers that shaped his color-blind philosophy.

On a road trip to play against the University of Maryland, my father was turned away when the team checked in to their hotel. The manager instructed them that the "black boy" could not stay there. My twin sister, Karen, and I never heard this story until my father was on his deathbed. One of his teammates called and asked me to put the phone to his ear. He wanted to apologize for never talking to him about the incident. It turned out my father spent the night at the home of the Maryland team's coach. The next day, he played the game of his life, scoring the most points and landing the MVP slot.

My daughter is growing up in very different circumstances. Through hard work, my husband and I have been successful in our careers in the financial sector. I remind her virtually every day that the life she's living is not something we inherited but something her father and I built. It came from both of us being fearless and putting aside our negative energy. We try to only see the rainbow, not the rain.

After high school I earned a track-and-field scholarship to the University of Virginia. I had my sights on training for the 1984 Olympics, but a pulled hamstring got in the way. After college, I faced a decision—move to Oregon to begin training for the 1988 Olympics or go to New York and start living my life. I chose New York.

I never had a goal of working on Wall Street. But I looked around New York and saw a lot of people making a lot of money at that time. I wound up in the Chase Manhattan training program.

As a rhetoric-and-communications major, I hadn't taken a single math or economics course in college, so I took financial classes at night at Pace University. When I started knocking on the doors of Wall Street firms, I was advised to get an MBA. Harvard Business School was the only school I wanted to attend.

After I was accepted to Harvard, my father tried to talk me out of going. He was afraid I wouldn't succeed. But his lessons about being fearless ran too deep. My mother always told us to "get in the front of the line" and to never stand behind other people. I knew I would make it at Harvard. In

1991, I joined Morgan Stanley and found my niche in wealth management.

My daughter once asked me how I have the confidence to convince billionaires to trust me with their money. I told her they're all just people. They all have a heart and a stomach and two legs and two eyes. If you walk through life without fear, without being intimated by anyone or anything, you will go so far.

This is an important message that I share constantly with Lauren as well as the young women that I encounter at schools and organizations in the New York City area, including the Young Women's Leadership Network and the Lower Eastside Girls Club. It's powerful for girls to hear the story of how someone who looks like me made it on Wall Street.

I will never forget the time we had a group of young women from a mentoring program come to our apartment in the West Village for a gathering. One of them looked around and started crying. "I never knew black people could live like this," she told me when I asked her what was wrong. She thought only hip-hop stars, athletes, and actors could achieve such a lifestyle.

I invest a great deal of time and energy into mentoring and leadership programs, whether for women in business or girls from underprivileged backgrounds. The example that my husband and I have set about giving back to others has sunk in for my daughter. Lauren attended the ceremony when I was honored in 2015 by the Young Women's Leadership Network. While she watched me speak onstage, she sent a text message to her father.

"I want to do everything I can to help these girls," she wrote. "If it wasn't for Mom they would have no hope."

Where there is no struggle, there is no strength. My father's lessons about approaching life with courage, tenacity, and color-blind lenses live on in my miracle baby.

————

Kimberley Hatchett is an executive director and wealth management advisor for Morgan Stanley. She has ranked as one of Barron's Top 100 Women Financial Advisors every year since the inception of the survey in 2006.

Don't Land on It

CHERYL SABAN
Philanthropist—social activist

My children have seen me wear many hats over the course of my sixty-plus years.

I have been a model, a recording artist, an office manager, an executive assistant, a retail shop owner, a writer, a philanthropist, a psychologist, a United Nations representative, a jewelry designer, and a glass blower. I waited until I was fifty years old to earn a PhD in psychology, and I've written fourteen books. One thing my kids know from watching me: If you have a goal, figure out how to achieve it, and then roll up your sleeves and get to work. Don't stop until you get the job done!

One line that I used again and again while raising my children was: "Don't land on it." Essentially, the phrase to my family means: "Don't sweat the small stuff." Reserve your energy for the battles that really matter. And there will be battles.

This line has become a kind of credo for us. Most of the time, it works.

As mothers, we have enormous impact on the mind-set and moral compass of our offspring. It would be great if this information were spelled out in bold letters in baby guidebooks so that it would be crystal clear to us before we have kids.

But absent that advance information, sometimes the school of hard knocks can be a marvelous teacher. I spent a great deal of time in that particular university, with my two oldest daughters in the bleachers watching my every move. In the end, we all received a well-rounded education.

My daughters, Tifanie and Heidi, watched me grapple with two divorces, multiple careers, male-female power struggles, and the emotional fallout that I suffered after being raped when I was eighteen.

They saw firsthand that I became an ardent supporter of women's rights and other causes because of my experience. All four of my children—my three daughters and my son—are more equipped now than I ever was in my early life to occupy their gender space with grace, dignity, and a more equitable distribution of power.

I was a child of the 1950s. Growing up in San Diego, California, in a lower-middle-class neighborhood, many of the female role models I was exposed to were women in aprons showing off freshly baked cakes or the latest household-cleaning appliances. I was pushed to learn how to type and take dictation in preparation for a secretarial job. I didn't know what to reach for. I wasn't expected to have big dreams.

I discovered how difficult it was to go up against embedded stereotypes of male and female roles after I was raped at the age of eighteen. I had to deal with police and detectives who treated me as though I had brought the assault upon myself.

My rape occurred during the days of hippies and so-called free love. The police took one look at me with my peasant blouse and bell-bottom jeans, and I never had a chance. They made me a victim all over again. And they did this, despite the fact that they knew my rapist was a bad guy. Although I had fearfully agreed to testify against him in court, the police never found the perpetrator.

In those days, there was no such thing as organized psychological help for rape victims. I had to grapple with the psychological pain of sexual violence on my own. It took time—lots of it. But now I count myself as a survivor.

More than four decades later, I'm thrilled to look out at the sea of women who are heading corporations, advancing in the areas of science, technology, engineering, and math, and pursuing their entrepreneurial dreams at a rate that would have seemed astonishing to me as a girl. Yet our daughters still confront, with frightening regularity, rape and violence. There continues to be an astonishing disconnect regarding what is permissible social behavior for men and boys toward women and girls. This is a global pandemic.

I was appointed by President Obama to serve as a public delegate and special representative to the UN General Assembly in the fall of 2012. One of the most compelling conversations was about the scourge of violence against women and how to end it. One out of three women will be a victim of violence in her lifetime. And it is often perpetrated with impunity. Why? There is tremendous pushback around the world against women for wanting more education, more visibility, more autonomy, more power, more freedoms, and that resistance has been manifested, tragically, by violence. It needs to stop. We all need to be part of the solution, because the problem is everywhere.

Several years ago I wrote a book called *What Is Your Self-Worth? A Woman's Guide to Validation.* I created the Cheryl Saban Foundation for Women and Girls, with a $10 million endowment and the mission statement of helping women and girls take the next step up. I wanted girls and women to have access to health care, education, jobs, and to be safe. My foundation makes grants to various organizations that serve women's and girls' interests—via scholarships, microloans, and other means for many years. One of the grants went to the UN Women's initiative and together we're working to fight violence against women across the globe.

For me, giving back to our community is a natural part of life. I believe it is an honor to help others, and I feel I have a responsibility to do this, because I have been blessed with the resources to make a significant difference in the lives of so many women and children.

Through all of my ups and downs, the lessons I taught my daughters through my actions were to develop resiliency and a positive attitude and to find your voice. You need all of these tools to navigate life. I had experienced violence, so I told my daughters to be on guard—to be vigilant and to try to steer clear of situations that could be dangerous. My goal was just to keep them safe.

When I was finally totally secure with myself—aware of my strength, and making my own way—I was of the right mind-set to love and be loved in a balanced and harmonious way. It was at that point that I met the man I have been married to for more than twenty-seven years, the father of my son and youngest daughter.

As my oldest daughters came of age, I wanted so much for them to avoid the hardships that I faced at their age. I suggested that they hold off on marriage in favor of going to college. I wanted them to see the world, find their passions, and gain more worldly experiences. I urged them to take the time to be on their own and to get a sense of how individuality feels before they attach themselves to somebody else. My now-grown children have followed many, though not all, of my suggestions.

What we tell our daughters is of vital importance. However, it's just as important to teach our sons how to be the kind of men who can be a true partner in life. I'm lucky to have found my happiness with a man who acknowledges and celebrates the equality of women. For so many women in the world at large, that's still a hard thing to find in a man.

Today's world is a very different place from the Betty Crocker days of old, but challenges abound. Feminism is experiencing a kind of face-lift. After so many years, that's a good thing. Our daughters will use a different vocabulary to describe it—they'll devise clever new phrases to inspire us, to lead us in a new direction in the crusade for empowerment and gender equality.

———————

Cheryl Saban is a philanthropist, writer, and advocate for women and children, with emphasis on education and health care resources. She is a frequent speaker on women's issues and contributor to the *Huffington Post*. She serves as president of the Saban Family Foundation, and also sits on the board of directors for Girls Inc., Children's Hospital Los Angeles, the Saban Research Institute, and the Saban Free Clinic. She previously served on the City of Los Angeles Commission for Children, Youth and Their Families, among other affiliations. Her fourteen books include *Soul Sisters: The Special Relationship of Girlfriends, All About My Mother,* and *50 Ways to Save Our Children.*

The Value of Work

C. NOEL BAIREY MERZ, MD

Cardiologist

Work hard, do your job, and make the world a better place. These are the overarching, gender-neutral lessons that my three adult daughters recall learning from me during their formative years.

My husband and I didn't lecture them about gender equality, but the message appears to have gotten through. Research tells us that human behavior is shaped by actions rather than words.

My husband and I are cardiologists. We raised our family with a full-time nanny, and, as needed, a cook and drivers. We hired females and males for this domestic "women's work"— whoever was best suited to the job. We also paid a living wage with benefits as an indication of how much we valued the importance of child care and household work. Indeed,

185

during the years we were paying off our medical school loans, we had nothing left after paying the domestic expenses. While we could have paid less (as many do), we exemplified to our daughters that feminism means valuing all "women's work."

As a dual-professional couple, one of us was often absent attending to emergency patient care or professional meetings and other obligations that required travel. Our home life was busy, but we had the habit of eating breakfast and dinner together as a family. This often required leaving the hospital relatively early and bringing work home. We exemplified to our daughters, who were doing their own school homework, the values of commitment and achievement necessary for feminist self-fulfillment and self-sustainment.

Making physical fitness a priority was important. As a former athlete and a physician, I understand the health benefits of physical fitness. As a college athlete in the 1970s, I participated in the debate and welcomed the changes for women following the passage of Title IV. Subsequent research now demonstrates an inverse relationship between athleticism and victimization of women. Specifically, women who participate in sports are less likely to be raped (current national average one in five women) or suffer domestic violence (current national average one in three women). We actively supported our daughters in sports, and made it a family activity. We set the example and expectation that sports were an essential part of life and a contributor to feminist physical and psychological health.

My husband and I also made sure that we knew what our daughters were doing. When one of us was away for our professional duties, the other made sure to stay home, particularly during the teenage years. Causing great embarrassment to our daughters, I contacted other parents whenever a party, sleepover, or other function was being held. Our daughters (and their friends) knew that we cared about their behavior. We did not think we could prevent our daughters from participating in adult behavior (alcohol, drugs, sex), but I aimed to be a sounding board to the misogynistic messaging in traditional and contemporary adult behavior. Today's digital open access and societal transparency are associated with lower rates of child abuse and increased tolerance of homosexuality, so perhaps we can improve misogyny. As parents we called attention to misogyny and exemplified the feminist behavior we expected in our daughters as they faced adult issues.

There is no question that we do our best life work together with spouses, partners, colleagues, and friends. Mother Nature, in her wisdom, decreed that there be female and male in our species. Like yin and yang, Democrats and Republicans, North and South, we need both women and men to optimize our society and the world. Currently, compared to women, men are more likely to be unemployed, less likely to attend college, and more likely to die earlier if unmarried.

In sum, feminism is humanism. We cannot exclusively exemplify to our daughters behavior and attitudes that will help them understand what it means to be a feminist without also including men. In our actions and our words, we must try to show that true partnership requires mutual respect, love, and admiration, and that these are humanistic qualities necessary to make the world a better place.

C. Noel Bairey Merz, MD, holds the Women's Guild Endowed Chair in Women's Health and is director of the Barbra Streisand Women's Heart Center and the Preventive and Rehabilitative Cardiac Center at Cedars-Sinai Medical Center, where she is also a professor of medicine.

A Pinch of Ginger

ALEX GUARNASCHELLI
Chef—restaurateur—TV personality

Like any mother, I love doing special things for my daughter. I love making her favorite foods just the way she likes them, right down to how I cut it up for her on the plate. I am proud that at a young age Ava is bright and eager to learn so much from me. But I never appreciated how much she looked up to me as a role model until we had a heartfelt exchange one day over the breakfast table.

On this particular morning, Ava appeared in the doorway of our kitchen and studied me silently as I stirred a pot of oatmeal on the stove. She watched as I sliced a banana and covered it with brown sugar and cinnamon.

"Mommy, I like when you add some dry ginger," she said softly. I stirred in just a pinch. I didn't know she had ever seen me add ginger. I poured her oatmeal in a bowl and stooped down to hand it to her. The aroma of the hot oatmeal and the spices passed fleetingly between us. A smile of gratification crossed her face. She took the bowl and dug on with her spoon, scooping and smacking her lips as she ate.

"Mommy, are you an Iron Chef?" she asked, without lifting her eyes from the bowl.

"I am," I answered softly.

"Can I be an Iron Chef, too, if I practice?"

"Of course you can, if you want."

"I wanna be an Iron Chef, Mom, and I want to make things taste good like you do, Mom." Still she didn't look up from her oatmeal. I couldn't take my eyes off her.

What seemed like a quiet, everyday moment at home turned out to be one where I came to understand how much my daughter identifies with me. Imagine being just six years old and understanding the nuance of a little dry ginger stirred into oatmeal? Or appreciating the significance of my accomplishment as an Iron Chef?

I am proud to have joined the ranks of culinary superstars who have achieved Iron Chef status. I won the title in 2012 after competing on *The Next Iron Chef: Redemption* series that aired on the Food Network. Iron Chef competitions are no made-for-TV cakewalk. I went up against nine other highly skilled chefs and persevered in a series of grueling cook-off challenges until one by one the competitors were eliminated and I was the last chef standing in the show's famous Kitchen Stadium. Winning the Iron Chef jacket was, quite honestly, the most validating moment I have had in my career to date. It was also the hardest thing I have ever tried to achieve. My daughter witnessed that final competition and shared in my joy at the end.

Ava showed me that morning in the kitchen how much she had learned from my Iron Chef experience. When I stood up to return to the oatmeal on the stove, my daughter sprang into action.

"I want an egg, Mom," she said, reaching into the fridge to pull a large brown egg from the end of the carton. I handed her the pan and watched as she carefully put it squarely over the burner on low heat. She took a touch of butter and then swirled it around the pan (yes—she swirled the pan in the air, like a pro). She carefully cracked the egg and watched, almost astounded, as it spread and began to bubble around the edges.

She sprinkled on coarse sea salt and black pepper, dispersing the seasoning as evenly as her little fingers permitted.

"I like when salt gets on the yolk, Mommy," she explained. I slid a spatula under the lacy edge of the egg and slid it onto a plate for her. "Can you cut it up, Mom?"

Ava tilted her head up to look at me. I cut carefully around the yolk and cut the white into small pieces.

"Don't break the yolk, Mom, okay?" she said with consternation. She was worried that the yolk would break. She is, after all, a chef's daughter. I thought about the time when Ava was just three and a half and running around the Union Square Greenmarket in Manhattan, tasting all of the different heirloom tomatoes and gobbling up tiny strawberries.

She took the egg and ate the white parts first. Then she picked up her plate, bent over the runny yolk, and slurped the yolk as one would slurp the last bite of a hearty soup on a cold day.

"I like eating the yolk separately from the white, Mom," she shared.

"Why?" I asked.

"Because the yolk is so soft and yummy and the white has the crispy pieces." She was making me wish I'd fried one for myself.

"I love that you make me things that taste delicious, Mom," she said. On top of everything else, now she was articulating the depth of the emotional bonding we were experiencing. My heart soared. I knew I needed to offer her some words of wisdom.

"You know, getting good at anything takes lots of time and . . ."

"Practice, Mom," she said, finishing my sentence. "And you have to make lots of mistakes and learn from your mistakes and then you make some more mistakes and then you learn, right, Mom?"

Right, Ava. In her childlike way, she made everything so clear. In that moment I was surprised at how much Ava was learning and absorbing about life and the pursuit of flavor. But even more surprising is how much I stand to learn from her.

———————

Alex Guarnaschelli is a chef, author, and TV personality who is known for her frequent appearances on the Food Network. She is an advocate for the antihunger organizations Share Our Strength and City Harvest, among other charitable causes.

The New Best Friend

DANA WALDEN

Television executive

As a mother of two daughters, I have always tried to emphasize the importance of nurturing strong friendships, particularly with other women. For my daughter Aliza, the close female friendship she had with a classmate in third grade would bring great joy and great heartbreak, for both of us. But it provided a valuable lesson as well.

Aliza and her best friend, Charlotte, had been as close as sisters since they were born—literally. My husband and I met Charlotte's parents in the hospital as we were both giving birth. At the time, Charlotte's mother was my closest friend. We bonded over the experiences, both wonderful and anxiety provoking, of being new moms. Aliza and her best friend shared many interests and attended the same school. Our families frequently socialized together, and the girls were for the most part inseparable.

When Aliza was eight years old, I noticed that something was bothering her in the weeks leading up to a third-grade field trip. I couldn't determine exactly what it was but our normally carefree child seemed troubled by something, although she wasn't talking about it. My husband and I figured it was simply the routine ups and downs of childhood.

On the day of the trip, which I had volunteered to chaperone, I remember being rushed and wondering what I could possibly wear that would be both appropriate for a day at the Chumash Indian Museum with third graders and then meetings with television producers later that afternoon. Sometimes these small decisions take more energy than the ones I face running a studio.

It was a hot day in late spring, toward the end of the school year. The Chumash Museum in Thousand Oaks, California, was about a forty-five-minute bus ride away from my daughter's elementary school in Santa Monica.

From the moment Aliza got on the bus, I could see that something was wrong. Her best friend, her partner in crime since birth, was palling around with another girl. And not just enjoying another girl's company, but actively excluding my daughter, aggressively glaring at her from time to time before turning her attention back to an over-the-top demonstration of affection for her newfound best friend.

Aliza was confused and so sad. What had she done to earn this ostracism from her best friend? Whom would she sit with if not her best friend? On any other day, there would have been no doubt that she and Charlotte would have sat together, thick as thieves. She looked around to find a seat on the bus, panicked, her eyes welling with tears.

I was floored as I watched this unfold in front of me. I was as baffled as my daughter as to why it was happening. And as I witnessed this painful experience, I was overwhelmed by a desperate need to somehow fix it. I wanted to do anything that would have soothed the heartbreak I was watching Aliza experience.

When we got to the museum, Aliza hung her head and trailed behind the rest of the group as we did a head count and prepared the start of our program. I gave her a hug and asked if she was okay. She said yes but took my hand.

"I'm a little sad because Charlotte doesn't want me to be around," she admitted.

"That's crazy," I replied. "You and Charlotte have been like sisters. There's no way Charlotte would try to push you out of the way." Looking back, I don't know why it was my instinct to say that, as I saw clearly that Aliza was exactly right.

By this time our group was walking up a narrow pathway to enter the museum. The temperature was rising and so was the dust as the kids shuffled around the museum grounds. As I watched Charlotte continuing to glare periodically at Aliza, my maternal instinct kicked in. I could not stand by while anyone—even Charlotte, who was nearly a member of our family—was cruel to my daughter. But how should I handle it? Should I intervene? Counsel Aliza to confront her friend? I felt as unprepared for this situation as my daughter.

I started to get angry. I decided to call Charlotte's mom and ask her if I could talk to her daughter directly about the situation. When I reached her on the phone, my heart sank a little as I quickly realized that she was well aware of this situation between our daughters, and worse, seemed resigned to letting it play out. Being the hands-on studio executive I am, I knew I couldn't just stand by and watch. I had to do something, and Charlotte's mom gave me her blessing to talk to her about it.

I pulled Charlotte aside and asked her if Aliza had done anything to upset her or hurt her feelings. I tried to let her know, gently, that her behavior was hurtful to Aliza. Charlotte assured me that Aliza hadn't done anything. She simply had decided that this other girl would be her "new best friend," and until she felt confident the friend felt her commitment, she did not want to be around Aliza.

As I listened to this eight-year-old's logic, I realized that despite my best intentions, this was not a situation I could fix for my daughter. There was no way to force Charlotte to return to feeling warmly toward my daughter. Even if I could, didn't my daughter deserve a best friend who liked her without adult intervention?

As much as it killed me to admit it, I knew in an instant that I didn't belong in the middle of this relationship between two young girls. Charlotte somehow saw Aliza as an obstacle to her meeting new friends, and there was probably nothing Aliza could do to regain her affection. I realized that as much as it pained me not to try to "fix it" for my daughter, it wasn't my job to sort it out for Aliza and Charlotte.

I gave Aliza a big hug that acknowledged her feelings, and for the rest of the trip I pulled back. All I could do was offer her love and understanding. As painful as it was to witness it, I was grateful that on this difficult school day, of all days, her mother happened to be there.

The struggle with Charlotte had a profound effect on Aliza. It was her first major encounter in the frailty of relationships, and in many ways it prepared her for the dreaded yet inevitable interpersonal dramas middle school would bring. Aliza and I discussed the situation at length at the time, and for years afterward.

In the end, the experience of this abrupt rejection taught Aliza many things. She learned the value of having a wide circle of friends who can offer her a diverse range of experiences, so that she isn't vulnerable to the whims of any one person. Through the pain she experienced, she now intuitively understands the need to be sensitive to others. She also knows well the importance of choosing friends who care about her feelings. Choosing the right people in whom to entrust our emotions and vulnerabilities may be the hardest but most important skill we learn in life.

For me, it was a valuable lesson that, despite my impulse that day, sometimes children need to figure things out for themselves. Parents cannot, and should not, fix everything for their kids—that's helicopter parenting at its worst.

Interestingly, Aliza and Charlotte were eventually able to move past the third-grade drama and the two remain friendly today. I couldn't have dictated a better outcome for both girls.

Sometimes I wonder if I am teaching my daughter important lessons, or if it's the other way around.

Dana Walden is chairman-CEO of Fox Television Group and one of the highest-ranking female executives in the entertainment industry. She has played an integral role in developing some of the most distinctive TV series of the past two decades, including *24, Homeland, Glee, Modern Family, Bones, How I Met Your Mother,*

American Horror Story, *The Practice,* and *Ally McBeal*. She's been honored by the Big Brothers Big Sisters of Greater Los Angeles and the Legal Aid Foundation, among other honors. She sits on the board of the Saban Free Clinic, the UCLA Jonsson Comprehensive Cancer Center Foundation, the Los Angeles Zoo, and the homeless employment organization Chrysalis.

The Most Important Goal

MIA HAMM

Athlete-advocate

The years I spent playing soccer made me the person I am today. I learned how to work with others, how to focus on goals, and how to accept failure as a natural part of the pursuit of excellence.

In my professional career, I knew what it meant to be champion, as a player on teams that won the FIFA Women's World Cup in 1991 and 1999 and Olympic gold medals in 1996 and 2004. Since my retirement in 2004, I have devoted a lot of time to working with young women to help pass on the important life skills I gained through participation in sports.

I cofounded TeamFirst Soccer Academy in 2010 with my longtime teammates Kristine Lilly and Tisha Venturini Hoch. TeamFirst hosts three-day soccer clinics for girls and young women in various cities throughout the year. Kristine, Tisha, and I went to college together. We played on the US women's national team together, and now after many years and many games, we all are mothers to our own daughters.

Our goal with TeamFirst is to nurture a passion for soccer and for competing. We know that team sports is one of the best ways to build character and a strong sense of self-worth. We teach the fundamentals of soccer, and we also try to show our students that competing can be a lot of fun. It's stressful and physically challenging, for sure, but it is also exhilarating and energizing.

Kristine, Tisha, and I almost always had a good time just being with our teammates. That feeling of camaraderie and bonding was a source of strength, something that helped us achieve both on and off the field. Too often, the intensity of athletic competition can be intimidating to women. With TeamFirst, my partners and I try to help women and girls overcome their doubts and enjoy the thrill of being in the game. You can't ever win if you don't try.

I had to get this message across to my own daughter, Ava, not so long ago after she had a tough time during a soccer game. She was goalkeeper and used her hands while she was just outside the penalty box to grab the ball. She broke down when the referee called her for hands, so much so that she had to be taken out of the game.

My husband, Nomar Garciaparra, was there to comfort Ava in the moment. As a former Major League baseball player, he's had his share of heartbreak on the field. I was out of town, but Ava was still upset enough that she and I had a heart-to-heart about it in her bedroom when I came home the following day. I asked if she felt pressure from her coach or her teammates for getting the penalty.

"No, but it was a mistake, and everyone knows I made a mistake," Ava said. I could see how much it was hurting her.

Ava's reaction was totally in keeping with her personality. She is more competitive by nature, and more intense, than her twin sister, Grace. She enjoys being the center of attention more than Grace. Both sisters love to dote on their younger brother, Garrett.

As Ava and I sat on the wrought-iron twin beds in the room she shares with Grace, I told her about some of my challenging moments on the field. I explained that everyone makes mistakes, and that making mistakes is how you learn. In my speaking engagements around the country, I often talk about how sports teaches you how to deal with setbacks and disappointments with dignity and grace. In this case, my daughter was giving me an opportunity to see this principle in action.

I let my words sink in a bit. I was trying to walk a careful line between not making too big of a deal out of the incident while still acknowledging her feelings. I didn't want Ava to think I was really upset about her error on the field or that I was scolding her for having such an emotional reaction. I wanted her to learn from the experience, and I wanted her to stop beating herself up for an honest mistake.

I finally asked Ava if she could think of another way she might have helped her team after being called by the ref. She didn't hesitate.

"Just by getting back in the goal and trying harder?"

Ava could tell by the look on my face that I was proud of her answer. I think too often as parents we don't give our kids the benefit of the doubt that they can understand big-picture issues. Ava's answer couldn't have been more fantastic. I'd hoped she'd find the confidence to express that sentiment to me without prompting.

My life wouldn't have been the same without the knowledge I've gained on the soccer field. It's a privilege to be able to share those lessons with so many young women. I know firsthand, as a player and as a mother, that it really can make a difference.

―――――――

Mia Hamm has been hailed by ESPN as the greatest female athlete of her generation. She was a professional soccer player for seventeen years, earning two World Cup championships and two Olympic gold medals with the US women's national team. She was elected to the National Soccer Hall of Fame in 2007. Since her retirement in 2004, she has remained an advocate for Title IX and women's sports. She heads the Mia Hamm Foundation that focuses on promoting opportunities for women in sports and helping to raise money, and awareness of the need for bone marrow and cord blood donations, and transplants.

Just Listen

MARGARET ABE-KOGA

Politician—community advocate

"She's too sweet to be a city leader." That's how the local newspaper described me when I first ran for a city council seat in Mountain View, California, a midsized suburb of San Francisco that is best known as home to the world headquarters of Google.

Within a few years, that newspaper covered my election to the council and later my election as mayor in 2009. That early campaign was hardly the first time that I, as a five-foot-two Asian-American woman, faced the "sweet" and "nice" stereotype.

My career in politics and public service has been an effort to fight bias and serve as a voice for the underrepresented. But somewhere along the way, I became so focused on the goal of empowering other people that I wasn't able to see the need that was right in my own family.

As a child, my Japanese immigrant parents told me to keep my head down, don't ruffle feathers, and don't question authority. Just work hard. That's what I did growing up and for the most part, it worked for me. Teachers liked me and I did well academically. I got along with my classmates and was liked by all the cliques in high school.

My pleasant demeanor masked insecurities that came from growing up in a poor family. My father was a gardener; my mother worked as a kitchen helper for an airline. They worked hard but struggled with their limited English. As soon as I was old enough, I became their translator and handled their affairs—whether it was dealing with contractors on house repairs, negotiating with collection agents for the overdue mortgage payments, or my dad's clients who neglected to pay him for his service. But at the age of seven, I was never taken seriously. My parents had little defense against being taken advantage of by others.

These experiences fueled my quest to empower myself as a woman of color. I went to Harvard University and became active in public service and politics where I saw it was possible to make a difference for people like my parents. At first, I was perfectly happy working in the background helping others win elections and govern. But one day, a female political consultant whom I considered a mentor had a new assignment for me.

"Margaret, you need to stop letting the boys take center stage and get up there yourself," she said. At the time, I had just given birth to my first daughter. The fired-up feeling of being a mama bear with a cub to protect gave me the strength I needed to run for public office. I figured that after bringing a new life into the world, I could achieve anything. And now I had a mission to make the world a better place not just for me but for my child.

My daughter Aili was eight months old when I won my first election, for a county school board seat. Two years later, I started my campaign for city council one month after the birth of my second daughter, Aina. I lost that first council race—the time both the local newspaper and the firefighters union deemed me "too sweet and nice." But two years later I ran again and garnered the most votes of anyone running for the council.

Suddenly, I had a platform to effect change. I spoke out against the racist who told me to go back where I came from, the anti-Semite who went after my Jewish colleagues, and the business interests who threatened our precious wildlife with plans for enormous real estate developments. I was always vigilant about the growing divide between the haves and have-nots in our community. In time, I became so comfortable speaking out that I felt no one could stop me. No one except my girls.

I wanted to instill in my daughters a sense of compassion for everyone in our community. I've been troubled by the issue of growing income inequality and our struggles to find solutions to this crisis. My discussions within the family often became angry rants against the rich and powerful. I lectured my daughters on how fortunate they were and how grateful they should be for their privileges. I told them they should fight for others to have similar opportunities.

As I vented my frustrations, I failed to see the internal turmoil that was affecting Aili. She was being bullied and abused. Rough play with a group of her friends eventually turned to physical violence. They rifled through her cell phone and started calling her names.

At first, Aili wouldn't tell us what was going on. But we knew something was wrong when tearful Sunday-night breakdowns over going to school on Monday started to become a regular occurrence.

It all came to a head one night after we got home from a trip with her Girl Scout troop to a homeless shelter where the girls helped serve a meal. I mentioned to Aili that I wished that her troop would do more service projects rather than outings strictly for fun. Suddenly, she blew up at me.

"Mom, this is why I can't talk to you about my problems, because you criticize what I do," Aili said. "You talk about how grateful we should be for what we have because other people don't have as much, so I feel like I am being self-centered to have the problems I have and my problems aren't important enough to talk to you about them."

I was speechless, shocked by her words. I realized that my laser focus on empowering and assisting others had the effect of stifling my girls. All of a sudden, the only thing that mattered to me was my daughter and the pain she had been quietly enduring. It was time to open my ears and just listen.

When Aili finally shared with me all that had been going on, the tears began to flow like waterfalls. "It's been so hard," she said as she cried. I held her as tightly as I could.

Perhaps it was consolation that later Aili told me she did learn from watching me, that she had to put her foot down and not take it anymore. She worked up her courage to give up that group of friends and eventually confront them about their bullying.

I realized that day that my girls have been a source of strength for me from the moment they came into this world.

My job as a mother is to reciprocate. It is only through an on-going dialogue of listening first, then talking, that we will grow our ability to embolden one another.

———————

Margaret Abe-Koga was one of the first Asian-American women to serve as mayor of a California city when she became mayor of Mountain View in 2009. Abe-Koga was elected to the City Council in 2006 after serving as an elected trustee of the Santa Clara County Board of Education. She has been active in numerous community and political organizations, including the Japanese American Chamber of Commerce and the Santa Clara County Democratic Central Committee. Earlier in her career, Abe-Koga held numerous posts on the staff of US Representative Anna Eshoo (D-CA), including that of a field representative focusing on immigration, housing, and civil rights.

Love Is a Verb

ROMA DOWNEY
Actress-producer

> An anxious heart weighs a man down but a kind word
> cheers him up.
>
> —PROVERBS 12:25

I learned what it takes to raise a beautiful child from my parents. I learned from their example, and I learned the meaning of kindness, faith, and love from the painful experience of losing them both.

My mother, Maureen O'Reilly, passed away when I was just a little girl, growing up during a time of the "troubles" in Ireland. Mom was my light, my joy, my whole world. When she died, it was as if someone just turned the lights out.

My father, Patrick Downey, lovingly stepped into the role of being both Dad and Mom. He was typically Irish, a man of few words, always quiet and thoughtful. He was a man of integrity, love, and kindness. Indeed, he was the kindest person I knew. He loved his family and God, and the faith we shared brought us such comfort as we learned to cope with our loss and a life without Mom.

Throughout my childhood, my dad would take time to pray with me. I can remember kneeling and praying together in our little kitchen in Derry with the sound of the rain on the windows outside.

When I finished high school, with Dad's encouragement, I went to college in England. It was a time of violence and political unrest in the North of Ireland and he thought there would be more opportunities for me abroad.

During my time at the Drama Studio London, I was homesick and I missed him dearly. I planned a visit to Ireland to see him, and we spoke on the phone the night before my trip to finalize my travel plans. I was so excited to see him.

"It's been raining here," he said, "and damp of course so I have hung your favorite yellow flannel sheets on the indoor clothesline to air." That was my dad—so kind and thoughtful.

I went to sleep knowing I was loved and looking forward to flying home the next day. But the unexpected happened. In the middle of the night, my father had a heart attack and died.

Heartbroken and devastated, I made the trip back to Derry the next day. When I arrived at our little row house on the hill, the silence was deafening. I walked into the kitchen and there hanging on the indoor clothesline to air were the yellow flannel sheets—the last kind act of a loving father. I held them to my face, breathed in their sweetness, and cried. His kindness touched me. I felt his love. And all these years later I still do.

I have told my daughter, Reilly, this story about the grandfather she never knew because I wanted to teach her about kindness. I use it to remind her that love is a verb and God is in the small stuff.

Reilly is a precious gift. When I was pregnant, I did not know I was having a daughter. When I heard the doctor say, "It's a girl," after she was born, my heart almost overflowed with love. I did not know I could love anyone this much.

In time I came to realize that all the parts of me that were hurt because my own mom had died, the parts that longed for a mother-daughter relationship, the parts that still felt the profound loss of my own mom, were healed by the joy of loving this beautiful baby girl. Reilly's birth was the *W* that filled the "hole" I felt inside me. She not only healed my pain and longing, she made me whole.

My daughter has been such a blessing in my life. As Reilly has blossomed into a beautiful teenager, I have shared with her all the stories about my parents that I can remember. She knows the value of family, of faith, and of the difference we can make in this world through our acts of kindness.

The embodiment of love is a family. As a young single mother many years ago, I met my future husband with his two young sons. When we married, we merged our lives to become one big family. That was a blessing for all of us.

The amazing Della Reese, my costar on *Touched by an Angel*, has been a mother to me these last twenty years, and a godmother to Reilly. I lost one mother and was fortunate enough to have been given another. Della is a blessing for all of us.

In spite of real loss in our lives, with faith and love we can heal and once again create wonderful new relationships. The lessons learned are at times painful. Loss is real, parents pass away, and hearts break, but the truth is that love never dies, not really. Love lives on through us. Not just in our memories but through our actions and the choices we make. In the way we live our lives we can make a difference.

These are the life lessons I've shared with Reilly, and she knows that I have tried to live my life to honor the memory of my parents. So many times I wished they were here and yet I know they are with me always.

I wish Reilly had been able to meet them, and yet I feel they are with her too. As their granddaughter, whatever she does with her life, whatever choices she makes, she has the chance to honor them. They live on through her.

Dr. Maya Angelou once made a beautiful observation about human nature: "I've learned that people will forget what you said, people will forget what you did, but people will never forget how you made them feel."

I will never forget the feeling I had when I held those yellow flannel sheets and breathed in the kindness infused by my father.

Love is a verb. It steps up and shows you that "I care" in a million different ways. When we step up and do something for someone else, and when we show kindness to others, we honor the past. We honor our creator and together we make the world a kinder place, for all of us.

I have always told my daughter to be kind whenever possible. And it is always possible.

———————

Roma Downey is an Emmy-nominated actress and head of LightWorkers Media, the production company behind the miniseries *The Bible* and *The Dovekeepers*.

An Act of Strength

CHIRLANE McCRAY

Activist-writer

When my daughter, Chiara, told me that she was struggling with depression, anxiety, and addiction, I had trouble processing what she was telling me. Her father and I knew that something wasn't right. But it was a shock to learn that our charismatic and caring daughter, who was beloved by her teachers, friends, and family, had such a serious diagnosis.

I felt everything you'd expect a mother to feel—afraid, sad, and determined to do *anything* to get her the help she needed. I also felt a fierce pride in my daughter. Because even though the last thing she wanted to do was call attention to a struggle that might make her look weak, and even though every second felt, in her own words, like a "bloody battle," she somehow found the strength to reach out to us.

As a mother, I have never wished more fervently for her to

hear me—really *hear* me—as when I told her, over and over again, that seeking help is an act of strength. And that I would be with her every step of the way.

I immediately dove into research, learning about mental illness, contacting mental health care providers, and piecing together the puzzle of resources required to get Chiara on the road to recovery. It wasn't easy to navigate. We had to trust the recommendations of people we didn't really know. We had to make big decisions based on faith.

We were lucky. We managed to find enough of what Chiara needed for her to begin her recovery. But I couldn't imagine how other families who lacked our resources could do the same. It was complicated. There was no system to guide our search for treatment options. While we were doing all that we could to help our daughter, it was clear to us that people were suffering needlessly from the lack of structure among the mental health facilities in the region.

It was clear to all of us that something had to change. In my capacity as first lady of New York City, I've made mental health my focus. Along with my husband, Mayor Bill de Blasio, we are working to make New York City a leader in offering treatment and support services to those who need help the most. The de Blasio administration has already increased spending for mental health by $500 million over the next four years. In late 2015, we released ThriveNYC, a plan of action to help our city move toward an effective mental health system. This year, we're gathering mayors from across the country to urge them to do the same.

In New York City alone, the scope of the crisis is shocking. Some 8 percent of New York City high school students report attempting suicide. The same percentage of adult New Yorkers experience symptoms of depression each year. Each year, 1,800 deaths and upward of 70,000 emergency-room visits among adults aged 18 to 64 can be attributed to alcohol use. Unintentional drug overdose deaths outnumber both homicide and motor vehicle fatalities, according to research by Thrive NYC.

Chiara is also turning her pain into a source of power. She is kicking butt at recovery. Somehow she finds time to advocate for young people facing similar challenges. And she plans to pursue a career in social work so she can help other families.

When I listen to Chiara share her story, I can't tell if she is following our lead, or if we are following hers. I have always been proud of her, but watching her these past couple of years has turned my motherly pride into a deep and sometimes awestruck admiration.

Seeking help is an act of strength. So is telling your mother that you need help. My love for Chiara and unwavering pride in her has only grown stronger. As our family pursues a shared vision of a New York City where recovery is possible for all, I hope that her father and I inspire Chiara half as much as she inspires us.

Chirlane McCray is first lady of New York City. She has worked as a writer, activist, and marketing executive. She served as a speechwriter in the early 1990s for David Dinkins, mayor of New York City, where she met her husband, Bill de Blasio, now the mayor of New York City. She is active with a range of nonprofit and issue-oriented organizations, including Edible Schoolyard Network, Hunter College center for autism research, The Feminist Press, and National Writers Union.

An Activist Upbringing

BLYTHE DANNER

Actress-activist

My daughter, Gwyneth Paltrow, grew up in a household where there was a constant undercurrent of activism. Of her many accomplishments—as an Oscar winner, as a mother, and as an entrepreneur—I'm most proud that she has carried on the tradition of being engaged with causes that are meaningful to her, and doing good things for others. It is what her father—writer-director-producer Bruce Paltrow—and I hoped to instill in our children.

In the 1970s and 1980s, gatherings were held in our home where a variety of speakers—including historian Arthur Schlesinger, Bella Abzug, and other members of Congress—would inform groups of actors and writers about defining issues of the day. When Gwyneth was about four years old, Carl Sagan came to speak about the threat of nuclear winter. She carried a banana around the room as a banner to show her support. She may not have understood the physics behind Sagan's warning, but she could feel the passion with which he spoke. Months later, her father's response to Sagan's call to action appeared in an episode of his NBC series, *St. Elsewhere*, thereby reaching millions of viewers.

During her teenage years, Gwyneth joined me to support pro-choice and reproductive rights policies through my work as a member of the national board of advocates for Planned Parenthood. Bruce, Gwyneth, and I joined with Planned Parenthood and others of thousands of activists in the 1989 march on Washington, spearheaded by the National Organization for Women. In 1997, her father received the first-ever Diversity Award, presented by the Directors Guild of America, for helping to advance the careers of minorities and women in Hollywood, perhaps setting the example for helping those most in need in our industry.

Together we collected signatures to fight the construction of a nuclear power plant on San Onofre State Beach in Southern California. That particular endeavor proved unsuccessful. However, now, more than twenty years later, that power plant is being shut down because of safety concerns. Later on, we advocated (this time, successfully) for the launch of curbside recycling programs in Santa Monica and New York City. In New York, our dear friend Christopher Reeve joined us to help get the message out. At one rally, he told children that Superman recycles, and asked them to get their parents on board.

Now that she's grown, Gwyneth has independently embraced a number of causes. One of those is serving as an executive producer of the biennial Stand Up to Cancer telethon that has raised more than $360 million to support cancer research since 2008. Her personal commitment is to the Oral Cancer Foundation and the Bruce Paltrow Fund, which helps inner-city residents receive free screening for oral cancer, reflecting her dad's interest in helping minorities.

Gwyneth lends support to a range of charitable organizations through Goop, the e-commerce and digital media business she launched in 2008 to help "share all of life's positives," whether it be a great recipe or travel tip or the perfect dress for spring. She has harnessed her celebrity to promote the importance of healthy eating and exercise, and she's been wonderfully outspoken about her determination be a committed mother to my dear grandchildren, Apple and Moses.

Gwyneth is funny, irreverent, and strong, with a tremendous capacity for empathy, wisdom, and love. It is telling that her closest friends today are ones she made in kindergarten and high school—a tribute to her loyalty and steadfastness.

In my early childhood, women were fighting for a fair shake at positions of power and influence. It makes my hopes for the future soar to see my daughter continue the fight for women to lead and set an example for the past and future. She steers through the inevitable critiques and complexities of her efforts to further the goal of women achieving power. I'm proud to call this fascinating and accomplished woman my daughter.

———

Blythe Danner is a two-time Emmy winner and Tony Award winner. She has been a longtime advocate for women's rights, environmental issues, and many other causes. Her Broadway appearances include *Butterflies Are Free, Betrayal, Blithe Spirit, Follies,* and *The Country House.* Her film and TV credits include *The Great Santini, Brighton Beach Memoirs, The Prince of Tides, Meet the Fockers, Columbo, Will & Grace,* and *Huff.*

The Rules

TANI G. CANTIL-SAKAUYE

California chief justice

Moms and judges have a lot in common. We recognize that clear, bright-line rules must be adhered to. But we also recognize that some rules lack precision. And sometimes there aren't any rules. In either case, we bring our training, our experience, our reason, and our intuition to help us illuminate the path forward.

Take Heelys, for instance.

If you observed children in the mid-2000s, then you know these sneakers with retractable wheels were all the rage. My two quiet, shy daughters would transform into spirit beings when flying around in their Heelys. Once, we were shopping in a big box store with expansive concrete flooring and I gave them the nod to take off.

As they carefully wheeled near me, other shoppers and store

employees smiled and asked where they could buy a pair for their children and grandchildren. The girls grew bolder and left my side, wheeling ahead of me and behind me. Soon, however, they returned to my side, upset and scared, near tears, with wheels retracted.

"What's wrong," I asked. They told me that a store lady had yelled at them. They were confused because earlier other employees smiled at them.

I huddled with them in an aisle. I said that the rules seemed unclear. And when the rules are not clear, it can be confusing, and as far as I could tell, I wasn't even sure the mean lady was right about the rule anyway. I told my girls that they didn't mean to break any rules and that they shouldn't be scared or shamed about using their Heelys. The yelling was wrong, I said, and hurtful. I suspected the clerk was wrong and even if she wasn't, I wanted her to try to yell at my children when they were with me. I encouraged them to wheel around the store with me. I wanted to draw out the mean lady. Very, very reluctantly and with much worry and uncertainty, my daughters used their Heelys once again, drawing not yells but smiles, once again, from onlookers and store employees.

Many years later, my daughters still talk about this incident. They remember their timidity and their confusion. They remember they tested the rules and shed their shame. They remember leaving the store feeling triumphant.

Of course, sometimes the rules *are* clear. But even when they are, they can be followed strategically. Take basketball, for instance.

When they were younger, my daughters were tall for their ages and played center positions. They were scratched, stepped on, shoved, elbowed in the ribs, and occasionally knocked down. Of all the basketball rules, I taught my girls, the most important one is this: You get four fouls; on the fifth foul you are taken out of the game. Rules are meant to encourage appropriate behavior and if that doesn't work, then the rules are meant to punish poor behavior. In a rough game, I told my daughters, when you are getting kicked around and the referees are asleep at the whistle, then use four of your fouls. I'll keep track of them, I told them. Use the rules to your advantage; don't waste opportunities. They didn't.

Finally, some things should never have rules. Like career paths. When I became the Chief Justice of California in 2011, both young and seasoned lawyers wondered what kind of calculated path I followed to become the first ethnic minority and second female to hold the position of chief justice in the state.

Truth be told, I didn't have a plan. But along the way, I met lawyers who saw the future of the bench and bar as something other than patrilineal institutions. I am a beneficiary of time and circumstance—and of male and female lawyers and judges—who saw the future and me in it.

After law school and the bar exam in 1984, my only plan was to get a job. With no leads, no connections, and no holds barred, I applied everywhere.

When a temporary opening at the district attorney's office was offered to me, I sincerely knew I wanted to be a deputy district attorney—whatever the job entailed. And where exactly was the courthouse again? Little did I know that as a prosecutor I would fulfill a lifelong dream: engaging in merit-based arguments and getting to have the last word. It was a dream come true for a well-mannered, Filipina youngest child with two big dominant brothers. I threw myself into trial work with such relish that I bemoaned the weekends when court was closed. Trial preparation and trial work gave me the confidence I needed, the experience I lacked, and the resilience to interpret the word "no" as "find another way."

Working as a deputy district attorney and participating in supportive bar organizations, I came to believe that anything was possible. I ignored advice that I couldn't get a job in the governor's office because I didn't have government law experience. I didn't calculate my odds. When I did get the job, I immersed myself in the work of the executive and legislative branches. I was appointed to the bench when I was thirty years old. I have been appointed to four levels of the bench by three different governors. I accepted each appointment thinking it would be my last.

During my trial court tenure, I became a wife and a mother. For a few years I put the legal community on hold and went deep undercover into nursery school, Brownie troops, basketball, and gymnastics. I let everyone know that I was putting family first and they should too. Although I knew my résumé would no longer look like a male judge's résumé, I look back on those years with unbridled joy. In each new position, I was sorry to let the last position go.

As I reflect on my path, I'm able to offer some very simple career advice to my college-age daughters: Ignore the rules of the common career trajectory. Work hard. Maintain a good attitude. Serve the public—and never forget to follow your inner Heelys.

Tani Gorre Cantil-Sakauye is the 28th Chief Justice of the State of California, and is the first Filipina American and the second woman to serve in that role. As leader of California's judicial branch of government and chair of the judicial council, she has been focused on improving the public's access to justice, increasing efficiency, transparency, and accountability, and revitalizing civic learning and engagement.

The Cooking Lesson

SHEILA BAIR

Financial expert—author

My daughter and I have forged strong bonds while cooking together. The arduous process of designing our dream kitchen gave Colleen an important lesson about sticking to your vision, even when the experts are rolling their eyes.

Colleen, then thirteen, and I sat at our contractor's gray metal conference table, hunched over a huge sheet of white paper crisscrossed in thin blue ink. The contractor and kitchen designer watched us in silence as we pored over every detail of the plans they'd developed for the kitchen in our vacation home. The blueprints seemed exact to the specifications Colleen and I had painstakingly developed after years of trying to practice the culinary arts in a cramped, 10-foot by 12-foot kitchen that was short on counters, cabinetry, stove burners, and refrigerator storage. This was to be our fantasy kitchen. No corner would be cut; no desire left unmet. We would have yards of counter space, two sinks, six stove burners, three ovens, and a refrigerator as big as a Mini Cooper.

So specific were we in our wants and needs throughout the design process that our professional designer had felt somewhat left out. Fortunately, she had not taken offense at our preconceived ideas of a cooking Shangri-la. Instead, she had willingly deferred to our dictates with good humor, even when our ideas deviated from accepted kitchen design norms. She now restrained herself as we discussed the optimal placement of the stovetop. Near the fridge where we could quickly grab and transfer eggs, milk, butter, and such into a simmering pot or pan? Or near the ovens, where the frittatas we so loved to make could easily be transferred from burner to oven?

Finally, she couldn't take it anymore.

"A lot of people like to put the stovetop on the island," she said. "That way, when you're cooking you don't have your back to your guests in the great room."

Her hand hovered over the spot on the blueprint where the kitchen area dissolved into the vaulted living space. She had a point. Colleen and I spent a lot of time in the kitchen, but my husband and son did not share our enthusiasm for food preparation. Having a kitchen that opened into the living room was our solution to family togetherness. Scott and Preston could read, play Scrabble, talk politics, or whatever while Colleen and I had fun in the kitchen.

"What do you think?" I asked my daughter.

The designer grimaced. I couldn't blame her. I was asking a thirteen-year-old to second-guess her opinion. I glimpsed the contractor rolling his eyes.

"Putting it on the island makes some sense," I continued, realizing that the designer had a point. "It will be easier for us to talk with Dad and Preston when we are preparing meals. And easier to talk with our guests when we are cooking for a party."

Colleen's cheeks flushed. She looked furtively at the designer, then gave me a look, half-resentful, half-pleading. I could tell that she thought the adults were ganging up on her.

"I really want to know what you think, little bear," I said, and I meant it.

"We picked out that great backsplash for the stove, remember?" she noted. Yes, I remembered. We'd searched for hours to find just the right fleur-de-lis tile design to serve as a backstop for the formidable Thermador six-burner we planned to install.

"And the pyramid ventilation fan," she continued. "The tile and the fan. They're so pretty, and we won't be able to use them if we put the stove on the island."

"That's true, sweetheart," I replied, a little disappointed that she was basing her arguments on cosmetic grounds. "But we need to focus on what will make the kitchen most functional, especially when the family is together or we are entertaining."

She furrowed her brow and began rubbing the ring on her finger—familiar gestures when she felt stress. I didn't want to pressure her, but we needed to make a decision. This was one of the final, unresolved issues, and construction would start soon.

I was about to give this one to the planner. But before I could announce my decision, Colleen rejoined the debate.

"We don't cook over the stove that much," she blurted. "We spend most of our time chopping and dicing. And we need a big counter space to make pies and pastries and things. The island is our biggest work space. If we put the stove on it, it will be cut in half."

"That's true," I said, picturing myself rolling out a piecrust at one end of the island, while she cut and pureed fresh pumpkin at the other.

"And if people are sitting around the island, it's not safe to have a hot stove. They might burn themselves," she said. Her confidence was gaining momentum. "How do we serve them? We don't want to lean over an open flame to hand them a plate."

More good points, I thought, now imagining myself serving crab bisque and fresh bread to Colleen and her friends with the soup pot simmering safely on the counter behind me.

I looked to the planner for possible rebuttals. She shrugged and said not a word. Perhaps she did not want to get into a debate over kitchen design with a thirteen-year-old. Or perhaps she appreciated the merits of Colleen's arguments as much as I did.

"Okay," I said. "Stovetop stays where it's shown on the plans now. Next to the fridge."

The planner smiled at the contractor. He rolled his eyes again in return. They probably thought Colleen was the most indulged teenager on the planet, with a hopeless pushover for a mom.

But as we wrapped up the final details with the designer and the contractor, I was happy to have had these tough decisions settled by the best-made argument. Colleen had prevailed by being thoughtful and prepared. I was won over by her reason and her assertiveness. And I was very proud that she was capable of standing her ground.

Sheila Bair is senior advisor to the Pew Charitable Trusts. She also serves on the boards of Host Hotels, Banco Santander, and Thomson Reuters. The veteran banking and regulatory executive headed the Federal Deposit Insurance Corporation from 2006 to 2011. She is the author of several books, including *Bull by the Horns: Fighting to Save Main Street from Wall Street and Wall Street from Itself*, and a columnist for *Fortune*.

The Tables Turn

RUTH W. MESSINGER
Nonprofit executive

Now that my daughter is grown, I realize how much she has informed my understanding of what it means to be a feminist and a leader. As she has matured and become a wife, a mother, and a professional, she has dealt ably and head-on with not only sexism, but racism and homophobia, and I have learned from her. In truth, Miriam has been my teacher more than I have been hers.

It's no secret that women of every generation, for more than a century, have wrestled with the tensions of having a family and having a career; being a mother and being an independent person. Navigating the messiness of these conflicts—and witnessing my own mother and daughter navigate this messiness too—has often given me pause, raised questions about when change happens and how, and forced me to think anew on issues I thought resolved.

My mother once told me—when I was an adult—that she was not sure that her choice to work when she had young children was "okay" until—decades later—she saw me make the same choice. My children, similarly, saw me making choices—to be on a public stage as an elected official, standing up for people's rights. They adapted well and often helped. But sometimes, I now understand, they might have wished that I was doing less in the public sphere and more at home.

As I made my choices and wended my way in politics it might have looked easy. But I had plenty of trying experiences with bias and discrimination during my political career in New York City. Often sexism gnawed at the edges and chewed through to the center of my work. When I expressed an opinion, I was often dismissed as being "rude," "pushy," or "hysterical." Once, when I requested a public hearing about a piece of legislation I'd drafted, a powerful male colleague responded by saying, "Of course you can have a hearing. I can never say no to a pretty girl."

I remember the challenge of talking to my daughter about these experiences so that she would know the problems that existed, be prepared to confront them, and be ready to move beyond them. She had a T-shirt, which I loved. On the front it read: "For a woman to be half as good as a man, she needs to do twice as much work in half the time." The back was punctuated with: "Fortunately, this is not difficult."

That message encapsulates the perspective I shared with her then: first, hard work pays off; second, sexism is a perennial setback; and third, humor helps. But, sadly, when I addressed these issues with Miriam—and with her brothers—I see now that I was too quick to suggest that the situation would improve dramatically with time and that life would be different when they came of age. Unfortunately, things may be different but the problems persist, which means we need, collectively, to be doing more to make change.

When it came time to apply for college, Miriam wanted to go to Harvard, where I had gone. I cautioned her about the university's mediocre reputation on women's issues and about the paucity of female faculty. But Miriam was unfazed, ready to take on those challenges and the others she would face, and much more ready than I had been to see the ways in which these and other inequities were built into the system. They required more than glib humor to be eradicated. And she is doing much of that work.

Today, Miriam is a lesbian mother and hardworking professional providing consultative services to not-for-profit organizations that are seeking to address some of these problems not only out in the world but in their own corridors. In her work and in her life she strives to be a better parent, a better professional, and a determined fighter against the ravages of discrimination based on race, class, and sexual orientation. She thoughtfully examines who she is and what she wants to do in the world. She takes risks, urges others to take risks, to reexamine the premises with which they approach the world, and to do more to make change in their lives, in their communities, and in broader society.

I hope and believe that Miriam and her brothers learned something from my efforts to deal with family, manage a fulfilling work life, navigate relationship challenges, and make broader social change. I know I am continuing to learn from her to do more and do it better, to be able to tell a more complete story of who I am, what I care about, and how to lead with dignity.

———————

Ruth W. Messinger is the president of American Jewish World Service, a nonprofit organization dedicated to improving the lives of people in the developing world.

The CEO of Cupcake Management

NORAH O'DONNELL

News anchor

I've tried to teach my daughters to be confident in their pursuits and the decisions they make. But how do you teach them to really take charge?

I think the key lies in encouraging the development of leadership skills at an early age. And who knew that a three-year-old's birthday party could turn into the ultimate classroom?

It was my younger daughter, Riley, who was turning three. When the time came to light the candles and sing "Happy Birthday," the children—aged three through five—were, rather predictably, undisciplined. In what was apparently an instinctive move, my older daughter, Grace, started directing the children to take their seats and choose a cupcake. I was a bit embarrassed in front of the other mothers that Grace was essentially ordering all the other kids around.

Just as I was about to apologize, my dear friend Elizabeth Moeller turned to me and said, "Wow. Grace has such executive leadership skills." We both laughed. I realized what she could also have said was, "Wow. Grace is really bossy."

It didn't fully dawn on me how important this moment was until I met Sheryl Sandberg, the COO of Facebook. I was interviewing her about her book *Lean In* for CBS News' *60 Minutes*. Sheryl wrote about how she was called "bossy" as a child, and how that specific word made her feel self-conscious for some time. Among Sheryl's recommendations for getting more women into leadership positions is the idea that we positively reinforce what have been perceived historically as "unfeminine" qualities—including assertiveness and decisiveness, which are often encouraged in boys. She also suggests that we stop describing our daughters in pejorative terms like "bossy."

Now when my daughter exhibits confident or authoritative behaviors I say, proudly, that she has "executive leadership skills" or acts like "a little CEO." I even made up T-shirts for my girls that say "I Have Executive Leadership Skills."

I thank my friend, Elizabeth, for constructively labeling Grace's talents at such an early age. As Elizabeth always says about that birthday party: "Grace was directing cupcake management."

The sibling-rivalry dynamic among my daughters and their brother, Henry, also provides plenty of instructive opportunities for everyone in our family. Even when it comes to something as routine as swim-team practice.

I want all of my children to love sports. Competition is one of the best ways to learn that hard work and practice yield positive results. So I jumped at the chance to sign them up for swim team even though at ages five and six they could barely make it across the length of the pool.

Practice came twice a week along with the inevitable whining about being tired or the water being too cold. Another constant was Grace's insistence that she always get to go first for the lesson with the swim instructor.

Grace's siblings usually relented. But one Tuesday, Grace's younger sister, Riley, decided she wanted to go first. I tried to defuse what I sensed could quickly escalate into a conflict by delaying a verdict, saying, "Well, let's decide when we get there."

By the time we reached the pool, both Grace and Riley had dug in. I was forced to issue my ruling, which was: Grace always gets to go first, so it's Riley's turn this time.

At this point, Grace stalked to a corner and crossed her arms across her chest. "I'm going first, or I'm not going at all," she fumed.

"Well, those are not the two options," I replied.

"I'm going first, or I'm not going at all," she said again, emphatically.

At this point, I realized there was a teaching moment at hand. I could easily tell her she was acting spoiled or was headed for a Time Out. But it occurred to me that there was something much more profound to be learned.

I started slowly, saying: "Grace, I really like that you want to go first all the time. Your passion to always be first is really awesome and will serve you well in life. I also really like that you feel so strongly about swimming and are so competitive! But in this instance, insisting that you have your lesson before Riley is not that important. She really wants to be first this one time. It's important to learn to compromise every once in a while in order to be successful and to keep other people happy. Plus, she's your sister!"

I thought that was a pretty clever talk.

Grace's response? "I'm going first, or I'm not going at all."

By that time, the substance of the disagreement was effectively moot, as Riley had already jumped in the pool. I turned and walked away from Grace, hoping that she'd cool down and that something might change.

Grace never said anything about my motherly pep talk. But after about five minutes she retreated from the corner, sat next to me, and waited patiently for her turn.

What do I think the takeaway message is? Now, rather than impulsively punishing what looks like bad behavior, I try to talk through and reinforce what might be my girls' developing grit and commitment to causes in disguise.

I pause and consider the moments in which my daughters show incredible tenacity and passion for what they believe in, and ask myself, "How can I nurture these traits and channel that determination in a positive way?" And then I hope my message to them gets through before I'm absolutely forced to issue a Time Out.

Norah O'Donnell is a journalist and cohost of *CBS This Morning*.

Hot Flashes

DONNA DE VARONA

Athlete-broadcaster

I am not one for labels. After delivering a speech to a private school on how sport empowers women, I was asked a telling question.

"Do you think of yourself as an athlete or a woman?" My response? "I think of myself as a human being."

I have discussed the subject of feminism with my daughter, Joanna. I made sure she understood that her opportunities have come from the work and collaboration of others who made huge sacrifices. She tells me that not many of her generation identify with the term "feminism." Because they were not part of the trailblazing efforts of past generations, they do not feel ownership of the movement or the word.

But the history is not lost on Joanna. She is constantly frustrated that no matter how progressive our culture has become, women still face a double standard in almost every aspect of our lives.

I have shared with her stories of what it was like for me as an aspiring athlete in the 1960s, and how hard it was for her grandmother, Marty de Varona, to only realize some of her dreams through her daughters' accomplishments. My father, Dave de Varona, was a Hall of Fame football player and rower for the University of California. He was an avid supporter of his children, but it was my mother who fought daily for us. She always told us, "You have to fight for a seat in life," and she meant it.

Joanna has noted that although she learned in school about how women achieved the right to vote, there was no mention of the far-reaching impact of the Title IX law and how its passage in 1972 mandated equal opportunities for women in education and in sport. She is frustrated that the work of the Women's Sports Foundation in fighting for the enactment and enforcement of Title IX is barely a footnote in feminist history.

And no matter how far we've come in other areas, the state of our physical appearance is an issue that challenges so many women.

My relationship with Joanna was taken to a new level when I was held captive by the onslaught of hot flashes. These episodes always seemed to hit during the dead of winter, when she waited for me in the endless car pool line outside her school. Dressed in a Catholic school uniform—and inexplicably forbidden to wear warm tights under her prickly wool skirt—she could hardly wait to climb into my toasty vehicle. Except that I often felt like I was sitting inside a furnace. My windows would be rolled down and the air conditioner on full blast. No words were needed, except for me to remind her to remember these moments and laugh out loud when it happens to her.

And then there is the big no-no, the taboo subject that we can't resist discussing even though we know we shouldn't: "How do I look?" In the context of a world flooded with images of impossibly thin women, this can be a hard question.

Joanna is almost six feet tall. She is strong, self-assured, and stunningly attractive. It should not matter that she is not a size 6 or a size 8. She jokes with me that the only guys who are interested in her are too old or too short, but her humor hides deeper feelings. I often remind her that I didn't get married until I was thirty-eight.

Since childhood Joanna has loved acting, singing, and performing in school and community theater productions. In pursuing her goal of becoming an actress, people who know better constantly tell her she must be thin, thin, thin to make it in the entertainment industry.

My sister, the talented actress and director Joanna Kerns, is more than my daughter's namesake—she is one of her role models. My sister and I have discussed with Joanna our own weight battles and the struggle of riding the thin-fat roller coaster. The younger Joanna puts in long hours of training at the gym to handle the fight on her own terms.

It took two auditions, but my daughter was accepted into London's Royal Academy of Dramatic Arts following her graduation from Catholic University of America. She firmly believes that knowing the classics—Greek plays, Shakespeare, Ibsen, Chekhov, and more—is imperative to an actor's success.

Now that she is going out on auditions, I want it so much for her that my heart aches. When she performs, I cannot breathe. I frequently remind her, and myself, that she has chosen an unpredictable profession where disappointment is part of the deal, but that she should never give up on her dreams.

At this stage of her life, Joanna is intently career-focused, yet she remains sensitive to those around her. Recently, she accompanied me on a trip to Boston for a Special Olympics International board meeting. I headed to Switzerland from Boston to deliver a speech in Lausanne.

Joanna had to leave before me for her job in theater with the Nederlander Organization in New York.

When I returned to my hotel room in Boston to pack, I was touched to find yellow note cards scattered around the room. Taped to my bathing suit a message read: "Mom take time out to swim, you always feel better when you do." Another read: "Because you forgot your toothpaste I have left mine for you," and another reminded me not to forget my cell phone charger. The last one I found after I unpacked my suitcase upon arrival in Switzerland.

"Mom I know your speech is going to be great, just make sure you do not speak too fast. I only wish I was with you to hear it because I always enjoy listening to you."

The rush of joy I felt in finding these heartfelt expressions of love gave me a very different kind of hot flash. I'm saving those note cards.

———

Donna de Varona is a two-time Olympic gold medalist in swimming and a pioneering sportscaster, who was the first woman to cover the Olympics on television in 1968. She is an advocate for women's sports, a member of the US Olympic Hall of Fame, and an active supporter of the Special Olympics. She is a cofounder and past president of the Women's Sports Foundation.

Rachel's Turn

NANCY JOSEPHSON

Hollywood talent agent

My daughter, Rachel Stern, was voted the girl most likely to be a CEO of her high school graduating class.

This made me happy on many levels. It was proof positive that I have passed on to her the ambition and drive that my mother and father gave to me. And I was gratified that my daughter had the benefit of attending a school that was forward-thinking enough to have a "most likely to be CEO" designation. It sends a great message to all students.

Rachel logged many accomplishments in high school, but if anything clinched the "most likely" title for her it was the fact that she was instrumental in helping the school pull off an incredible conference focused on young women during her senior year. And she did it while battling mono.

The brainchild of one of her classmates, the It's My Turn

conference attracted 1,000 girls from all over the Los Angeles area. The day was packed with inspiring speakers, highlighted by an appearance by Lady Gaga to talk about bullying. Rachel was a key player in making the event happen, and she powered through her responsibilities to the very end even though she could have easily bowed out because of her illness. But after working so hard with her classmates to make the event happen, she wasn't about to let mono stand in her way of seeing it through to the end. That's CEO-level leadership.

Rachel has no shortage of ambition now that she's an undergraduate at Brown University. Watching her reminds me of being a young lawyer in Manhattan in the early 1980s, fresh out of Harvard Law School. It was the height of the Yuppie era and I walked to work every day in my power suits and sneakers.

Back then, I was very ambitious and focused, but I also knew I wanted a family. I didn't think about how I was going to manage both, I just barreled ahead. I eventually moved to Los Angeles and became a talent agent. In 1998, I became the first woman to earn the title of president at one of the big Hollywood agencies, International Creative Management. I was promoted to the post as a copresident alongside a man twenty years my senior. The announcement got a lot of attention outside of Hollywood industry circles because of the first "woman president" angle.

I worked hard to climb that ladder, and I've always tried to be the best agent I could be for my clients. It's a work ethic that I got from both my parents. My father is a self-made businessman and my mother immigrated to the United States from Norway during World War II. After my parents divorced in 1970, my mother went to work in a publishing house. I saw her flourish at her job. She would come home, change into comfortable clothes, and tell me about her day. I had never seen her happier, and I'm sure that was a large part of why I grew up expecting to be a working woman. After my time as a lawyer, I followed my father into the cutthroat world of agenting.

For my daughter, I've tried to demonstrate that it's possible to have a fulfilling personal life as well as a successful career. Finding ways to blend work and family, when appropriate, can enrich experiences all around, especially if you love your job as I do. Being a talent agent can be highly stressful, but it can also be a lot of fun.

From the time they were small, my three kids frequently visited me at my office. I always tried to take them to work-related activities that I thought were appropriate. Being the child of a Hollywood agent means you grow up on the red carpet, attending movie premieres, award shows, TV tapings, charity dinners, and many other glitzy events. You get accustomed to being around celebrities in a way that brings an important perspective about the nature of fame.

I've also gained great insight into my work through my kids. I knew that the Disney Channel was about to become must-see TV for my daughter's generation when I heard about a new show, *Lizzie McGuire*, from a girl in our school car pool. Her mother happened to be the head of the Disney Channel. I was able to arrange for Rachel's Brownie troop to visit the set of the show just as it took off with her friends. That experience was a fun perk for Rachel and her troop, but it also made her feel that I was listening to her and valued her taste in matters that intersected with my professional life.

Rachel now has her eye on a career in the entertainment

business. She's already thinking strategically about how to get there, and she's made it clear she'd like to avoid dealing with the high level of stress that I faced at times. I remind her that I have always found it helpful to turn to female friends who all seem to be dealing with similar issues. Instead of breakfast meetings, we like to use the time to walk or hike while we compare notes.

As Rachel sets off on her own path, I'm excited to watch this fabulous young woman grow and achieve her goals. She and I are already comparing notes on our experiences. As a Mother's Day present, she wrote a response to this essay. In her words:

If there is one thing that my mother does exceptionally well—one thing that I'm willing to admit to her that she does exceptionally well—it's her ability to balance work with family. It was very rare that my mom wouldn't be home for dinner, or be able to put me and my two brothers to bed at night. If she had to go to a work event, she made sure to leave us notes on our pillows that we would find right before bedtime, so it was as if she were actually there.

If she had to go to a client's taping of a show, we would make it an opportunity to have mother-daughter time. During the taping, I would schmooze as only a talent agent's daughter could, and she would put on her agent face. Afterward, we would go to dinner and it would just be normal time for the two of us.

Some of my friends talk about how they can't wait to be married. I never understood this. My feeling is I can't wait to graduate and start working. I know I'm going to have to work in a job being somebody's slave for a few years for no money until I can start to move up. But ultimately, I am going to be a major figure in the industry, making a lot of money and enjoying my job by the time I'm thirty. I am a very driven person, and I like to be the boss. This is something that I definitely learned from my mom.

See what I mean about the gift of ambition?

———————

Nancy Josephson is a partner at WME-IMG, the world's largest talent agency.

The Making of Makers

SUKHINDER SINGH CASSIDY

Internet executive–entrepreneur

When I was about eight, my father sowed the seeds of my career as an Internet executive and entrepreneur by teaching me how to do his bookkeeping.

My father, Jagmohan, owned a small medical practice where he and my mother, Amar, worked together serving patients for more than thirty years in Canada and Africa. My father didn't believe in hiring accountants. He taught my two sisters and me how to study his checks and bank statement each month and meticulously record his expenses into a large ledger by hand. It took hundreds of hours for our whole family to get the books in order each year in time for income tax season.

By the age of twelve, I knew how to do his full tax return. A few years after that, I created an Excel-based accounting system that was much more efficient. When my parents were well into their seventies, they took a computer class to learn Excel so they could run the system after I went off to college.

My father was also a lover of business, innovation, and technology. When I was in second grade, he helped me build a working model of the human eye for our school science fair. In the sixth grade, he came into my classroom with a working model of blood circulating through the heart and body that he built at home. A few years later, the first time I ever heard of AOL was when my father excitedly called his stockbroker to tell him, "We have to buy this stock." He had fallen in love with the promise of the Internet before I even knew what it was.

Fast-forward twenty-five years; I have spent the past two decades invested in the business of technology. I've worked as a senior executive at Google, started my tech career with Amazon, launched three start-ups of my own, and ran another as CEO. I have a healthy family with three children I adore: Ryan, Kenya, and Kieran. But it is my daughter, Kenya, who especially loves to create. In her I see the spirit of an entrepreneur, just like my father. My opportunity as her mother is to fuel her ambition.

Kenya loves writing stories. When she was as young as four, the two of us began finding images on Google, with her weaving a story in real time that I would type as she told it to me. Together we'd place the pictures exactly where she wanted them in simple Word documents. Those stories piled up in my computer until we found a self-publishing program via Blurb to create *Kenya's Book of Short Stories* at the age of seven. She loves to gift it to family and friends but also learned to promote it and price it and put it up for sale.

We've created coffee-table books featuring Kenya's artworks using another Internet-based publisher, Artimus, which is a friend to every parent who can't bear to throw away their child's art. Every year since she was in preschool, we've carefully sat down to choose her favorite pieces of art, sent them off to Artimus for processing into a book that we get to further design online. Seeing the physical product of her creativity, designed by her, never ceases to bring a smile to her face. She loves the service Artimus provides so much that she once starred in an online video about them, explaining the product on my ecommerce site Joyus.

At various times over the last three years, Kenya has dreamed about starting different businesses. As an animal lover, I once discovered that she had written down pages of meticulous instructions for a new pet store online game she thought would be better than the one she was playing. We talked about needing to find a developer to help bring her design to life, but she later lost interest.

This summer Kenya invested time and effort into an online cupcake business she launched with her friend Madison—kandmcreations.net. These days she talks about owning a ranch or being a writer.

I have no idea if Kenya will grow up to become an entrepreneur as an adult. What's most important, I believe, is that she sees starting a business not as a distant, daunting, and unimaginable goal—but as an inevitable, beautiful, and entirely attainable means of expressing who she is and what she has to give to others.

Starting a company is not about what you do; it's a vehicle for expressing who you are and how you channel your unique contribution to the world around you. Our job is to ensure that every girl we raise knows this is her opportunity too.

Sukhinder Singh Cassidy is founder, chairman, and CEO of the online video shopping network Joyus. Before launching Joyus in 2011, she was chairman-CEO of the ecommerce venture company Polyvore and served as the CEO in residence at Accel Partners. From 2003 to 2009, Singh Cassidy was a senior executive at Google, including serving as president of Asia-Pacific and Latin American operations. She has held executive posts at Amazon, British Sky Broadcasting, OpenTV Corporation, and Merrill Lynch. She serves on the board of directors for Ericsson, Tripadvisor, and J. Hilburn.

I Am the Tooth Fairy

JEANNE NEWMAN
Entertainment attorney

My daughter, Hillary, is one of the most confident and fearless people that I know. She can glide into a room of accomplished strangers, introduce herself around, and leave with at least one new friend. She uses a flying trapeze for workout sessions, lived for a week below the poverty level in order to blog about the experience, and she has a Siamese fighting fish for a pet. But she wasn't always this way.

When Hillary was four, she had a mortal fear of the tooth fairy. It was perplexing. Her girlfriends would practically extract their own teeth to hasten visits from the tooth fairy. But Hillary kept her teeth in for as long as possible out of dread. The thought of some wispy creature wafting up to her perfectly pink bedroom, sticking a bony arm under her pillow, and exchanging a tiny tooth for a quarter was terrifying to her.

At first I tried to console her by suggesting that she leave the tooth in a package by the door to her room. That worked for a molar or two, but soon the thought of an apparition in her doorway kept Hillary up for an entire night after a tooth fell out. I then suggested that we leave the next lost tooth in the mailbox. That way, I reasoned, the tooth fairy didn't even need to enter our house. But still, the idea of the fairy flying around outside caused Hillary another sleepless night.

I finally realized that the fairy fantasy had outlived its purpose. What really was the point of perpetuating a silly myth that was making my daughter miserable? Why was I forcing her to be brave about an imaginary creature when there were going to be so many other challenging real-life situations that she would have to confront? I decided to take Hillary into my confidence and share with her one of the first big truisms of adulthood.

I took her into my bedroom and shut the door. We sat down next to each other on her bed and she knew I was about to tell her something big.

"Okay, Hilly. There is no need to be afraid of the tooth fairy, because I am the tooth fairy. I have been the one who takes your teeth from under your pillow and replaces them with quarters."

A look of enlightenment and amazement passed over her face. I felt bathed with relief that her anxiety had been abated and that I had finally handled the situation well. We hugged.

As I started to get up, she asked if she could ask me one question. "Of course," I said.

"What other houses do you do?" Hillary asked.

We laughed after clearing up this momentary confusion. Ultimately, from this mother-daughter moment, Hillary came to understand that the situation that was frightening her the most—in this case, the tooth fairy—wasn't as scary as it seemed once we talked it over.

The insecurity she conquered through the tooth fairy experience came to mind several years later when Hillary was in seventh grade and was accepted into one of the first classes at the Archer School for Girls in Los Angeles. Archer had been formed three years before as an all-girls secondary school with a mission to teach young women in the ways they learn best, with an emphasis on building critical thinking skills, fostering intellectual curiosity, and collaborative learning.

The head of Archer, Arlene Hogan, asked me what I hoped the school could do for Hillary. I explained that while Hillary seemed shy and quiet to others, I knew she had a strong inner voice that was just waiting to be let out. I challenged Arlene to help Hillary find that voice. The results came faster and louder than I ever expected.

The first year at Archer was amazing for my daughter. Her class was so tiny that she was encouraged to play two varsity sports and join the robotics team. And the school itself was so young that she and her classmates had real influence in setting the rules and on administrative questions. That year the students distributed at least thirty petitions protesting everything from the types of legwear allowed at school to the hot-lunch providers. By the end of the year, Hillary herself was sending around petitions relating to the number of inches that needed to be between boys and girls at school dances (zero) and the abolishment of length requirements for skirts in the uniform. No big surprise, but none of these petitions did much of anything to change the rules.

During this period she managed to find her way into a *National Geographic* magazine feature as a poster child for the 90210 zip code. She held her own in a debate with a well-studied rabbi on the existence of God. She argued with world-famous fashion designers about fashion trends. She was more than happy to express her opinion about anything and everything—whether the situation called for it or not.

That inner voice had gone from a whisper to a shout amplified by a bullhorn. As much as I'd wanted her to develop the confidence to speak up, clearly, things had gone too far.

As the school year drew to a close in June, Arlene called to see how Hillary's year had been.

"Great," I said, "but can you dial it back? She might be better off holding back just a little bit."

Arlene advised me that bringing out a girl's voice is not an exact science and that I would have to live with the results. And she reminded me that Hillary's behavior would inevitably modulate over time.

I've been happily listening to my daughter's distinctive voice ever since. Hillary is now the youngest member of the board of trustees of the Archer School. And I am convinced that one day she will be a spectacular tooth fairy.

Jeanne Newman is an attorney who represents prominent film and television writers, directors, and producers. She is a longtime partner in the Beverly Hills–based law firm of Hansen, Jacobson, Teller, Hoberman, Newman, Warren, Richman, Rush & Kaller, LLP.

Back in the Saddle

CHRISTINE BARANSKI

Actress

On a recent flight to London, where I was headed to shoot a film version of *Into the Woods*, I listened to the cast album of the Stephen Sondheim–James Lapine musical.

The opening lines of the song "No One Is Alone"—"Mother isn't here now / now you're on your own"—brought tears to my eyes.

The lyrics reminded me of the many times I left my two daughters when they were young to go off to work. How many of us working mothers leave the house hoping that one day they'll forgive us? Hoping that one day they'll understand that we were trying to set an example and instill in them the importance of independence, integrity, and strength of character—the qualities that will allow them to be on their own one day.

I've always encouraged my daughters to dream big, get a

first-rate education, and trust that hard, persistent work will ultimately pay off. "Aim high," I often told them, "but muddle through gracefully."

For my older daughter, Isabel, mud, in fact, was a key factor in one of those life lessons that occur at unexpected moments.

My girls grew up in a small rural town in Connecticut where my husband spent his childhood. Being country girls, their lives at a certain age revolved around horses. In spring, summer, and fall, they went off every day to an unpretentious local barn run by a no-nonsense woman named Bonnie. They loved nothing more than the smell of fresh air, liniment, and horse manure.

Isabel leased a large handsome horse named Moca. He was, of course, her surrogate boyfriend. Her fella. All her prepubescent energy, her passion and rapture, was channeled into that four-legged being . . . rather than a two-legged boy.

And Isabel had her work cut out for her because Moca was headstrong and stubborn; she took pride in her ability to tame his strong will. But the real measure of her success with Moca would come at the big autumn horse show, an auspicious event that required weeks of preparation.

Isabel felt an acute sense of anticipation, anxiety, and emotion leading up to the show, which took on an Olympian sense of importance in our home. I could only stand by and hope for the best. Best would be a blue-ribbon showing by Isabel and Moca. But just getting through the day without an injury would be a relief for a parent standing helplessly on the sidelines. Watching your child complete a series of jumps has more drama than a Broadway opening.

When the big day came, there was much ado for Isabel

about getting dressed, grooming the horse, getting the two of them to the right place, and being ready for the competition.

Alas, horses can be unpredictable creatures, especially this one. Isabel's fella decided to stop dead in his tracks on the first big jump, sending her flying. She was not hurt, but it was a rainy morning and she was covered in mud. She was stunned, humiliated, and exasperated. Her fella unceremoniously dumped her, after all that preparation, and on the first jump.

Isabel tearfully met me on the sidelines, angry and shaken, wet and muddy, and announced her decision to go home. She now hated that horse and declared that trying to tame him had been a big waste of time.

I let her vent in the car for a little while. Our home was only about fifteen minutes away. Carefully, I suggested that she reconsider the situation. I told her that this event, this experience, was no longer about a horse, a ribbon, or a defeat of any kind. It was actually a chance for her to reveal her true character.

I told her to take some deep breaths, go home, change clothes, and return in time for the next event. Getting back on that horse would be her real triumph. Life would indeed present her with thousands of such setbacks, big and small, I said. It was the exercise of character that mattered.

Finally, I assured Isabel that she would look back on this day with pride and humor if she got back in the saddle. She did, and Moca dumped her again. She remounted without hesitation, gave him a round of sharp whips on the neck, and after about six attempts finally got him over that series of jumps.

It was not a performance worthy of a blue ribbon, but she got a huge round of applause from the crowd that clearly recognized her pluck.

Today, Isabel laughs every time she recounts that muddy day, and she remembers it with fond detail.

Christine Baranski is an Emmy- and Tony-winning actress and costar of the CBS drama series *The Good Wife*.

Acknowledgments

I began the process of working on this book four years ago with
Cynthia Littleton. We've known each other for years as professionals but became friends after learning that we had much in
common. Over the course of this journey, seismic events have
occurred in both of our lives. We've leaned on each other for
clarity, advice, and comfort to a degree that went well beyond
our collaboration on this project. I could not have navigated
these times without her partnership, wisdom, and kindness.
She has been the literary lighthouse masterfully guiding this
collection of essays to port.

To Carolyn Reidy, leader of Simon & Schuster, thank you
for giving us this opportunity. You said "yes" before I even knew
what I was doing. Judith Curr, president and publisher of Atria
Books, and editor Greer Hendricks were always encouraging

and inspiring, never more so than when Greer opted to make a career transition, leaving the comfort and security of her longtime professional home for a new adventure. She embodies the spirit of what many of the women featured in *What I Told My Daughter* have expressed to their girls: live by the courage of your convictions, follow your heart, and go forth in confidence. Editor Dawn Davis accepted the baton from Greer and compassionately and patiently coached us across the finish line.

To Leslie Moonves, my boss, friend, and mentor, thank you for not throwing me out of your office after I talked your ear off more than twenty-five years ago! To my cherished friends and associates at CBS, thank you from the bottom of my heart for your unconditional love and support. I am one of the lucky ones.

Amanda Diedrich, my longtime assistant, you went above and beyond the call of duty. None of these pages would have been possible without your hard work, encouragement, and attention to detail. Bless you. Mike Campanizzi, thank you for your boundless enthusiasm and support.

To my children, Matthew and Alice, let me quickly write "I love you" before I dissolve into a puddle of tears. To my husband, Jerry, I am so glad I took the job as your assistant director forty years ago. You've been my hero ever since.

To my mother, Norma Carol Theresa Grau Ruth Tassler, I will never be able to express the depth of my love and appreciation for all the lessons you have taught me about life, love, and loss.

And to all the mothers who gave of themselves to contribute to this book, thank you for sharing insights on raising strong daughters. The emphasis you've placed on the importance of helping girls fulfill their potential and achieve their goals gives the next generation a license to lead. By lending your voices to *What I Told My Daughter,* you're encouraging future generations to start this important conversation early and never stop talking.

About the Authors

Nina Tassler has worked as an entertainment executive in television and theater for more than thirty years. After earning a degree in theater arts from Boston University, she began her professional career working behind the scenes at the Roundabout Theatre Company in New York City. She moved to Los Angeles, where she worked as a talent agent at Triad Artists before shifting into television development. In 1990, she began a professional association with future CBS Corporation chairman, president, and CEO Leslie Moonves that would span three companies: Lorimar Productions, Warner Bros., and CBS. After nearly twenty years at CBS, Tassler stepped down as chairman of CBS Entertainment in January 2016. Of all her accomplishments, Tassler is proudest of her marriage to actor-director Jerry Levine and their amazing kids, Matthew and Alice.

Cynthia Littleton is managing editor of television for *Variety*. An entertainment journalist for more than twenty years, she is the author of *TV on Strike: Why Hollywood Went to War over the Internet* and coauthor with Susanne Daniels of *Season Finale: The Unexpected Rise and Fall of the WB and UPN*.